The Reliable Boat

Douglas A. Low

With Confidence and Self-Reliance Become Master of Your Boat
Hard as a Solid Rock Against the Sea

HelmSafe Press

Jordan, New York

Copyright © 2015 by Douglas A. Low

All rights reserved

For information about permission to reproduce sections of this book, write to : HelmSafe Press
262 Clinton Rd
Jordan, NY 13080

Visit our Website: http://www.TheReliableBoat.com

Preface:

Do you want to master boating? Take command, take control, have the power. The only way to do this is to have a bulletproof, rock hardened vessel that will operate against all the wiles of nature. A rock on water; ready for battle.

A reliable boat can't be bought. It is created by a captain dedicated to the skills and knowledge that make it possible through the identification and elimination of the issues that can disable and destroy.

Machines are fallible and nature is cruel. Use those machines in nature, especially the sea and you are at risk. Your job is to minimize the risk so you and your boat will continue to maintain life and mobility.

The purpose of this book is to change the mindset of the average boater. A new boat is a beautiful thing. However it does not have the necessary capability to overcome many of the obstacles you are likely to encounter at sea. You have to build in that capability. There are methods and means for your boat to be more reliable. I want you to understand and execute them on your boat.

There is no such thing as a perfectly reliable boat but there is a capable captain. That's you. You are responsible for the success of each journey your boat will take. You need to continually increase your knowledge and skills.

Some of the analyses in the book are beyond the ability of individual boaters. I understand that. We will never get the reliability numbers for every part and be able to string them together to get a system reliability value. However if you understand the principles and use the methods spelled out in these pages you will increase the ability of you and your boat to handle what nature throws at you.

I'll do what I can but it's up to you.

Doug

Contents

HOW TO USE THIS BOOK _____12

The Intended Reader _____12

The Scope of the Book _____12

Parts You May Skip _____12

CHAPTER 1: WHY BE RELIABLE? _____15

The Questar _____15

Disasters _____17

What is Normal Reliability? _____18

Murphy's Law _____19

Chapter 2: Captain and Crew Responsibilities _____21

The Captain's Objectives _____23
    Keeping the Vessel and Crew Safe _____24
    Prevent Drowning _____25
    Keep Afloat _____26
    Keep Control _____26
    Know Where You Are and How to Get Where You Are Going _____28
    Prevent Fire _____28
    Vessel Configuration and Maintenance _____29
    Alcohol Use While Operating a Boat _____30

Crew Responsibilities _____30

CHAPTER 3: RELIABILITY ANALYSIS _____33

Reliability Prediction _____35
    Bathtub Curve _____35
    Redundancy _____38

Reliability Modeling _____39
    Reliability Calculations _____40

Reliability (Probability of Success)	40
Component "Series" Reliability	42
Multiple Component Reliability (Parallel)	42
Multiple Component Reliability (Series/Parallel)	43
Multiple Redundant Component Reliability	45
Propulsion Reliability	48
Engine	48

CHAPTER 4: A SYSTEMS APPROACH TO A RELIABLE BOAT 51

The FMEA Process – Identifying Problems	**52**
Identity the Potential Problems	52
Identify the Potential Solutions	53
Risk Management - Risk of Failure	**54**
Failure Mode Risk Analysis (FMRA)	**58**
Review of FMEA and Risk Analysis	58
Identify Potential Problems (Risks)	59
Identify Potential Solutions	59
Update the Risk Data	60
FMRA Boat Example	60

CHAPTER 5: STEPS TO INCREASE MARINE RELIABILITY 65

A Systems Approach to Preventing Engine Failure	**65**
Cooling-System Solutions	**65**
Raw Water Flow	65
Flexible Impeller Pump	66
Exhaust Manifold and Riser	67
Early Warning for Cooling System Problems	68
Cooling System Monitoring	69
Raw Water Flow Sensor	69
Exhaust Gas Temperature	70
Exhaust Manifold and Riser Surface Temperature	70
Heat Exchanger Temperatures	70
Cylinder Head Water Temperature	71
Thermostat	71
Ignition System Solutions	**71**
Points & Condenser	71
Other Ignition Component Considerations	72

Fuel Solutions _____ **72**
   Ethanol Fuel _____ 72
   Fuel Filter and Water Separator _____ 72
   How to Prevent Diesel Fuel Contamination _____ 73
   Fuel System Monitoring _____ 76
   Electric Fuel Pump _____ 76
   Spare Fuel Tank _____ 78

Starting System Solutions _____ **78**

Keeping Controls Operational _____ **78**

Electronics Reliability _____ **79**
   Electrical and Electronics _____ 80
   Dielectric Compounds _____ 80
   Conformal Coating _____ 82
      How to Put Conformal Coating on your Marine Electronics ____ 83

Charging System _____ **84**

Battery _____ **85**
   Emergency Battery Pack _____ 87

CHAPTER 6: PREVENTING AN EMERGENCY _____ 89

Fire _____ **89**

Fire Response _____ **90**
   Electrical Fires _____ 91

Fire Detectors _____ **92**

Wiring _____ **93**

Flood – Dewatering (Bilge Pump System) Reliability _____ **93**

Bilge Pump System Failure _____ **100**

Above Water Leaks – Rain _____ **103**

Adding Bilge System Strength _____ **104**

Bilge Pump Installation _____ **105**
   Bilge Pump Switch _____ 105
   High Water Alarm _____ 106

Bilge Pump Monitoring	106
Emergency Pumps	106

Thunder & Lightning Storms ... 107
    Thunderstorms ... 107
        Lightning ... 109
    Grounding System ... 110
    Bonding System ... 111
    Risk to Onboard Life ... 111
    Risk to Onboard Electronics ... 111
    Risk to the Hull ... 111
    Lightning Review ... 112
    Lightning Recommendations ... 112

CHAPTER 7: MONITORING ... 115

Bilge Monitoring ... 117
    High Water Alarm ... 118
    Bilge Pump Monitor ... 118

Water in the Fuel ... 118

Fuel Level Monitoring ... 119

Engine Condition Monitoring ... 119
    Engine Temperature Monitoring ... 119
    Raw Water Flow Monitoring ... 121
    Engine Oil Pressure ... 122

Filter Clogging Indicators ... 122
    Fuel Filter Clogging Indicator ... 122
    Oil Filter Clogging Indicator ... 122
    Air Filter Clogging Indicator ... 122

Battery Charge and Condition ... 123

Navigation Monitoring ... 123

CHAPTER 8: EMERGENCY PLANNING ... 125

What Happens in an Emergency ... 125

Plan ... 126
    Identify a First Mate ... 127

    Plan for Rough Weather _____ 127
    Minimum Supplies and Equipment _____ 128

Emergency Repair _____ **128**
    Leak Repair _____ 129
    Emergency Signaling _____ 130
    Loss of Control _____ 130
        Loss of Rudder: _____ 130
        Loss of Stern Drive Steering: _____ 131
        Steering with One Engine: _____ 131

Damage Control Boards _____ **132**

Running Aground _____ **135**

Prove It Before You Use It _____ **137**

Enjoy _____ **142**

BIBLIOGRAPHY _____ 143

APPENDIX _____ 146

    Minimum Supplies and Equipment Checklist _____ 146

Table of Figures

Figure 1: Sea Anchor or Drogue 27
Figure 2: Bathtub Curve 36
Figure 3: Reliability Curve 41
Figure 4: Series Model 42
Figure 5: Parallel Redundant Components 43
Figure 6: Series/Parallel Model 44
Figure 7: Operational Redundancy 47
Figure 8: Probability of NO Failure 50
Figure 9: Risk Factor Calculation 57
Figure 10: Electric Fuel Pump Wiring Diagram 77
Figure 11: Fuel Pump Sizing 77
Figure 12: Leak Rate from a Two-Inch Hole 98
Figure 13: Rate of Leak vs. Head (Depth) from a One-Inch Hole 99
Figure 14: Bilge System Placement 105
Figure 15: Closed Circuit Cooling 121
Figure 16: Collision Mats 129
Figure 17: Bungs 129
Figure 18: Keep Your Course with a Dead Engine 132
Figure 19: Damage Control Board Example 134

Table of Tables

Table 1: Captains Objectives 24
Table 2: Probability of Success for Various Components 46
Table 3: Typical Single-Engine Components 49
Table 4: Consequence of a Fault 55
Table 5: Likelihood of a Fault 56
Table 6: Definition of the FMRA Data Fields 61
Table 7: Captain's Objectives to Consequence Value Mapping 63
Table 8: Why Boats Sink 95
Table 9: Bilge Pump Sizing 105
Table 10: Lightning – What to do 112
Table 11: Monitoring Sensors 116
Table 12: Equipment and Supplies Checklist 146

How to Use This Book

The Intended Reader

The intended reader of *The Reliable Boat* is anyone interested in enhancing his or her boat's reliability. This book is especially suited for owners and skippers of offshore cruisers who take their passengers far away from homeport and away from shore because those onboard are placing their trust in the reliability of the boat and the ability of the skipper to get them safely where they want to be.

Owners of power boats, sailboats, and commercial vessels can use this book, as well. Another well-suited group is the small passenger boats that ferry their occupants to and from fishing grounds and sightseeing adventures. Many of these vessels are lacking in reliability, as you will see throughout the book, even those that meet all of their regulatory requirements.

The Scope of the Book

The goal of *The Reliable Boat* is to extend readers' knowledge of boat equipment, configuration, and operation to enhance their ability to get where they want to go and back safely without needing a tow. The book is particularly interested in the enhancement of boats beyond their reliability off the show room floor. It goes on to explore the skipper's responsibility and the theory of reliability, and provides specific examples of how to make any specific boat more reliable.

Included in this book is a detailed reliability analysis that you as an owner or a skipper can perform on your boats. It will show you how the boat is most likely to fail and what you can do about it. This part of the book is not for the technologically challenged, as it requires the use of a computer and web browser, and it requires you to know your boat's configuration and equipment.

Parts You May Skip

If you do not care about the background of reliability analysis, you may skip the first sections of Chapter 3: Reliability Analysis. If, however, you want to perform a reliably analysis on your boat, be sure to skim the parts that cover Single Component and Redundancy. Also, read the section on Failure Mode and Risk Analysis (FMRA).

Chapters 4 and 6 are stand-alone references to increase your boat's reliability.

Everyone should read Chapter 5: Preventing Emergency.

Contact me anytime about anything. I'd be glad to hear from you:

Doug@HelmSafe.com

Be sure to download Analysis Spreadsheet at:

(http://TheReliableBoat.com/ExtraStuff)

The spreadsheet is not for everyone but if you can use a spreadsheet and have a grasp of the analysis part of the book it will give you a good start to analyzing the reliability of your boat.

Also, go to http://TheReliableBoat.com There you will find more tips and techniques to make your boat the most reliable it can be.

Chapter 1: Why Be Reliable?

Roll on, thou deep and dark blue Ocean—roll!
Ten thousand fleets sweep over thee in vain;
Man marks the earth with ruin—his control
Stops with the shore. –Lord Byron

Entering open water brings the unanticipated to the unprepared. Through the real examples, analysis, planning, and equipment upgrades depicted in this book, you will better understand what can go wrong and how to be prepared for most equipment failures. Those who are prepared have the best chance of getting where they are going and returning safely without being towed.

The Questar

The owner of an 18-foot, open-bow motorboat, called the *Questar*[28], and one passenger were participating in a three-day fishing derby south of Shelter Island, Lynn Canal, near Juneau, Alaska, with about a thousand other vessels. It was an overcast, rainy day, and the wind was blowing at 25 to 30 knots. The seas were at 3 to 5 feet, but the skipper was able to keep water from spilling over the bow as he headed into the wind. The seawater temperature was about 55°F and the National Weather Service in Juneau had issued a small craft advisory for that area of the canal.

That day an unexpected tragedy occurred. At about noon, the *Questar* pulled up to a fish-packing vessel to unload its full load of fish. While the *Questar* was tied to the vessel, it took on water from boarding seas. As the *Questar* pulled away from the fish-packing vessel, its outboard engine sputtered and stopped. The captain tried multiple times to start the engine for the next 30 to 45 minutes as the boat, powerless, drifted toward Admiralty Island.

The water began to rise in the *Questar* because it only had a small-capacity bilge pump. The boat did not have an VHF radio, so the owner flagged down a passing boat and asked its captain to notify the Coast Guard of the *Questar*'s distress. Due to heavy traffic on channel 16, the captain of the passing boat had difficulty delivering the message, but eventually, he reached a Coast Guard auxiliary vessel and dispatched it to tow the *Questar* to safety. So far, everything seemed normal, and although the owner of the *Questar* had not expected the engine to fail, help was on the way.

The Coast Guard auxiliary vessel met the *Questar*, attached a line to its windless, which was high on the bow, pulling the bow lower in the water, and began the tow. The towboat operator didn't realize the owner of the *Questar* was mildly disabled and therefore a weak swimmer. The tow started OK but waves began to surge over the *Questar*'s bow, which swamped the small, open-bow boat, and placed the passengers in the high waves and cold water. Upon seeing what happened at the end of his 150-foot tow line, the towboat operator, reacted quickly and put the towboat into reverse, snarling the towline in its props, and losing the ability to rescue the *Questar*. The owner of the *Questar* got stuck under the boat and drowned, but the towboat operator was eventually able to save the *Questar*'s passenger.

In hindsight, there were multiple opportunities to save that life. The *Questar* began the day with a well-running engine, but its owner failed to heed advisories, have adequate bilge-pumping equipment, and or know the proper boat towing procedure. If the owner of the *Questar* had been better prepared, he would in all likelihood still be alive.

According to the U.S. Coast Guard [16], there is a 14% chance that someone will die if your boat swamps or sinks while underway. According to Boat U.S. [17], the number-one reason boats sink while underway is water over the gunwale. This happens if you cannot keep your boat under control in heavy seas or your bilge pump system cannot keep up with the rate of inflow. In other words, multitudes of mistakes and/or component failures increase the odds a fatality will occur on your boat. The job of the Captain is to minimize the odds of failure. This book will show you how to do that.

Anyone who has owned a boat for any length of time knows it can fail. Parts wear out, foul, or clog up and sometimes leave their passengers at the mercy of passersby, towboats, currents, weather, and time. So how likely are you to be stranded? How reliable is your boat? Is there anything you can do to make your boat more reliable? Can you actually guarantee your boat will be able to return to homeport on its own propulsion? The answers to these questions are in this book.

Disasters

Just as you cannot guarantee that a drunk driver will not kill you on your way to work, you cannot guarantee that you will return from the sea. The best you can do is increase your chances to near certainty.

If you get a chance to read accounts of what happens in boating emergencies, beyond these writings, gain experience from reading about other boat owners' failures. It will give you a new perspective on what can and does happen when you take your boat out to sea. A simple internet search for "disaster at sea," "boating accidents," or other related terms, reveals some pretty interesting stories.

In most boating emergencies where the boat suffers major damage or people die, three things become evident:
1. More than one thing goes wrong at once.
2. People panic, which adds to the problem.
3. There seems to be an acceleration of bad news. Circumstances become increasingly worse as the emergency progresses.

In any emergency involving a boat, bad news accelerates. One mishap causes another, and within a short period of time, you have a rip-roaring emergency. Plans are necessary to allow cool thinking and fast action to stop the acceleration.

A good plan results in clear thinking. A good plan helps keep problems down to one at a time, reduces panic, and gives you more control. This book will teach you how to create a well-thought-out plan, which is a lot easier to follow than a plan sketched out in the heat of panic.

These chapters will also help you determine how reliable your boat is and how reliable it should be. This book will also teach you how to maintain the components of your boat to increase its reliability. It is my goal to help you understand which components and features will ensure that you get where you want to go and get back again safely once they are added to your boat. Drawing from my background in military equipment design, I will provide an objective analytical approach to marine reliability, safety, and longevity.

What is Normal Reliability?

Your boat's manufacturer is good at building a boat that will be reliable for 3 to 5 years after an initial starting period. This figure is based on what is known as Mean Time Between Failure (MTBF) of most commercial components. This figure represents how long an individual component is designed to last under normal operating conditions, a concept I will discuss in more detail later in this book.

For now, just know that the manufacturer of your boat has little incentive for increasing your boat's reliability beyond 5 years because the average new boat buyer will purchase a new boat before the 5 years have passed. Boat manufacturers probably also assume that anyone who becomes stranded in his or her boat can call for help and be towed to shore. This is "normal" reliability. They rightly put the responsibility on the skipper without providing any means of fool-proof reliability themselves. If the military took this approach, it would leave sailors stranded during the most critical times of battle.

The military requires its vessels and operations to be measurably reliable based on the equipment and use of that equipment. In a mission-critical system, if the system fails, the mission for whom the system is being used also fails. A mission-critical system will leave nothing to chance. The military calculates the failure rate of each component along with the entire system. The result is a measure of how reliable the system is. The military then determines how long it will take to fix the system, including the time it takes to get parts. That final result is called "availability."

The military breaks its systems down into life-critical and mission-critical systems. An example of a life-critical system is a nuclear bomb, which could cause massive loss of life if it fails. Both the military and its contractors typically require a system to be available for operation for a certain percentage of time so they can determine how reliable the system is. That does not mean that nothing will break; it just means a particular system is still operational. Perhaps the failure caused a redundant component to be used while the primary component is being repaired. For mechanical components, the military knows how long each component is expected to operate, along with the consequences if the component fails.

Normal reliability is not good enough if you are going on a 3-month cruise across the South Pacific. If, on the other hand, you are taking your boat out on a sunny day, with no wind, to water ski for ½ an hour, you can afford to be a little more lax. You need a system that has reliability compatible with the type of boating you do.

Murphy's Law

Apply Murphy's Law liberally: "If anything can go wrong it will." (http://dmawww.epfl.ch/roso.mosaic/dm/murphy.html) Other web sites about regarding Murphy's Law, as well, and I suggest you look them up. Sayings like the following are all part of Murphy's Law:

Mother Nature will always find the hidden flaw.

Matters always get worse under pressure.

Everything bad will happen at once.

Things left alone will go from bad to worse.

If you drop buttered bread, it will always land buttered side down.

There is no end to things that can go wrong.

No battle plan survives contact with the enemy.

A failure will not occur until the unit has passed final inspection.

The expert in a crowd is the one who predicts the highest cost and the longest schedule.

The only perfect science is hindsight.

Some of these sayings, like the buttered bread, are not technical accurate but provide a ring of truth. For example, there is an end to things that can go wrong, but it is a very long list.

When applying Murphy's Law to the subject of boating, it really means:

> *If it's possible that something bad will happen, it will eventually happen, and probably at the worst possible time.*

You must stop the bad from happening. Although you can never guarantee that nothing will go wrong, you can reduce the probability of something bad happening. If nothing is done to reduce that probability, then your chances of multiple things going wrong increases, and that is when you will need Devine help. As a boat captain, you will usually be able to handle one thing going wrong, but you will find it much harder to handle multiple problems at once.

I have spent my career designing and building complicated military electronic systems. I have watched as well as given many demonstrations of these high-tech projects. The gizmo being demonstrated can be working perfectly one minute, and then as soon as the Admiral or General steps into the room, the system will crash. I have seen it time and time again. It is probably the result of a nervous operator, but it does happen. Something bad will happen if you don't remove the possibility of it happening. This requires boat captains to think of everything that can possibly go wrong onboard and take steps to lower the probability of any of those things occurring.

Chapter 2: Captain and Crew Responsibilities

"The safety of a yacht and her crew is the sole and inescapable responsibility of the captain, who must do his best to ensure that the yacht is fully found, thoroughly seaworthy, and manned by an experienced crew who are physically fit to face bad weather. He must be satisfied as to the soundness of the hull, spars, rigging, sails, and all gear. He must ensure that all safety equipment is properly maintained and stowed and that the crew know where it is kept and how it is to be used."

-- OFFSHORE RACING COUNCIL (ORC)
REGULATIONS GOVERNING MINIMUM EQUIPMENT
AND ACCOMMODATIONS STANDARDS

In the middle of winter (end of December) disaster struck in the Atlantic Ocean just off Charleston Harbor [29]. A father, two sons, and a nephew were sailing their way home after purchasing a used 34-foot sailboat. The slight threat of a storm added to the thrill, as each was experienced at the helm and therefore not worried. With a stiff wind at their backs and the warmth of home strong on their minds, they were all excited to be exactly where they were. The 60-hour trip required a steady pace if they were going to get home on time. Still, they saw no big problem.

Toward evening on the second day, however, they left the Inter-Coastal Waterway (ICW) on an unplanned route. The wind started to pick up, and the waves increased to 3 to 5 feet. The family members seemed fine, though; they just needed to stay vigilant and keep moving. Hitting a rock jetty was not part of their plan.

The *Morning Dew* was a 34 CAL sailboat equipped with an auxiliary diesel engine. It was apparently in seaworthy condition, most likely operated as expected, and could easily handle the 3- to 5-foot waves that day during a small-craft advisory. The crew members knew they had a 60-hour trip and needed to make better time if they were going to make it home on time.

The skipper only had a compass and charts for navigation—no GPS or Loran. There were few or no visible landmarks at night in that area. They also did not have the necessary clothing to keep warm during high winds, rain, and low temperatures. The skipper was not familiar with that section of coastline, and he had three young boys onboard and no other adult to take over if he got cold or tired.

The Coast Guard received an unintelligible mayday call around 2:00 a.m. The watch stander responded over the radio, but got no answer. He assumed it was just a radio check or someone wanting information but changed his mind. Around that time, the *Morning Dew* struck the rock jetty on the north side of the channel.

Based on the 54 F water temperature, they could have survived anywhere from 1 to 6 hours. The operator, who was already cold and probably at least slightly hypothermic, would have lasted the least amount of time.

Two of the four bodies washed up on the beach the next day, and the Coast Guard eventually found the others. The mother in the family had to identify the bodies and the voice in the distress call. Most likely, the family members would have been fine if they had used more caution and kept to the safe inland route.

The beginning of this story might be similar to other stories. A man buys a boat, and he and his teenage sons were anxious to get it to their home port. Every day the boat was left at its old home marina was more money spent. Considering the family had an extra-long weekend, it made more sense to sail the boat home than pay exorbitant fees to have it transported. In this story, however, the new owner, his 2 teenage boys, and a teenage cousin died as a result of poor preparation, poor navigation, and poor judgment on the part of the owner.

- They should have stayed in the ICW as planned.

- They should not have gone into the open ocean during a small-craft advisory, at night without good navigation capabilities.
- A simple GPS with a couple of predefined waypoints would have saved the 4 lives.
- The captain should never have gone into the ocean at night without someone to take over if he became incapacitated.
- This list goes on and was spelled out in great detail by the National Transportation Safety Bureau so others could read it and not make the same mistakes.

The Captain's Objectives

The Captain of any boat has multiple objectives. The major ones are listed in Table 1. The list is in relative order from most to least important. As you can see, the first objective is to keep everyone alive and the last is to make everyone happy. When the table says prevent death and loss of property, it means onboard prevention as well as protecting the lives of others around the boat or affected by the wake.

Depending on your particular circumstance, you might put things in a little different order, but these will hold up pretty well. Preventing the boat from sinking, for example, is slightly more important that preventing the boat from catching fire because a captain can't fight a fire as long as the boat is above water, but once it slips below the waves, it doesn't matter anyway. This is one reason among many that the exact order is not as important as the objectives themselves.

Table 1: Captains Objectives

Captains Objectives	
Prevent Death	1
Prevent Loss of Property	2
Prevent Sinking	3
Prevent Fire	4
Maintain Lights	5
Maintain Mobility	6
Maintain Lubrication	7
Maintain Fuel Level	8
Keep Vessel From Grounding	9
Navigation Redundancy	10
Maintain Critical Redundancy	11
Maintain Bilge System Performance	12
Maintain Electrical Circuits	13
Maintain House Battery	14
Maintain Speed Control	15
Maintain Direction Control	16
Maintain Full Performance	17
Maintain Full Speed Capability	18
Maintain Ease of Starting	19
Maintain Engine Performance	20
Maintain Cooling	21
Keep Frustration Level Down	22
Make Passengers Happy	23

Keeping the Vessel and Crew Safe

The primary responsibility of the Captain of any boat is the safety of those on board and the safety of those around the vessel. This includes crewmembers, visitors, swimmers, water-skiers, occupants of other vessels, and anyone who can be affected by the boat or even the wake of the boat. The secondary responsibility of the Captain is to maintain the condition of the vessel and other vessels and property around his or her vessel. This is a serious responsibility and should not be taken lightly.

The owner and operator of the boat share this second responsibility. The owner is responsible for making sure the vessel is equipped and properly maintained. The operator is responsible for the operation, and therefore, must have control. The operator should also be aware of the maintenance status of the vessel. The following story illustrates the shared responsibilities of a boat owner and operator, as well as the response of the government in the face of recreational boating disasters.

A rental vessel went aground on a Florida coral reef due to a combination of bad weather reporting, a poorly maintained vessel, (the VHF radio failed and an anchor rode was frayed and broke), and lousy judgment on the part of the operator. The state of Florida takes its coral reefs seriously and levies massive fines upon all who violate them. Guess who had to pay? The weatherman? No, the owner and the operator were both fined $50,000 each for the grounding. I guess the court figured the vessel and skipper should be ready for all circumstances, including the unexpected. That is the way it is and should be. The captain should be ready for all contingencies. He or she should expect the best, but be ready for the worst.

Prevent Drowning

The Captain and crew should consider wearing a Personal Floatation Device (PFD). According the U.S. Coastguard [18], the greatest risk of loss of life is when a passenger falls or is ejected overboard. This happens more than you want to know. The best prevention is to wear a PFD. PFDs for each passenger should be available immediately. Little children should always have on a suitable PFD whenever they are on the boat. It is the Captain's responsibility to ensure that happens.

If the captain says, "Wear your PFD," then the passengers should put it on without complaining. If the Captain says, "Do not go up to the bow," then the passengers should not go up to the bow. If the Captain says, "Sit down," then the passengers should sit down. It is not an ego trip, but rather an issue of safety.

The Captain should take precautions to keep people from harm's way. He or she should take into account the passengers' age, strength, and ability to swim, along with the sea and traffic conditions. It is too easy to be thrown overboard if the boat hits a large wave from a passing vessel.

The bottom line is that everyone onboard needs to obey the rules.

Keep Afloat

If a boat sinks while underway, there is a 14% chance that someone will die. One of the Captain's most important goals is to keep the boat above water. More boats sink each year than you might think [18]. In 2002, 559 boats capsized, 348 boats flooded and swamped, and 335 just sank. There are several reasons why boats sink:

- Water over the gunwales
- Leaky thru-hull fittings
- Raw water-cooling system leaks
- Exhaust leaks
- Grounding
- More...

The bilge system is one of the most critical systems on the boat. There should be redundant pumping capability and high water alarming at a minimum. There is no maximum. Ideally, any bilge system should include the pumping system, the alarm system, emergency power, and emergency pumps directly coupled to the engines. None of this is too much because boats do sink and people die when boats sink.

The Captain must make sure the boat has emergency capability in order to keep the vital systems working.

Keep Control

The goal here is for the Captain to keep the boat moving forward toward its intended destination. This requires engine or sails and steering control. In heavy seas, the best strategy is for the Captain to keep the bow into the wind. This requires working engines and the capability to control the thrust vector. Things are going to break when they are needed the most, and that happens when the most stress is placed on the boat's components.

The Captain must have a plan to keep control if systems fail. If the throttle cable snaps, if the rudder fails, and even if all else fails, the Captain needs a plan and he or she needs to implement that plan quickly.

The ultimate contingency plan for bad weather is to put out a sea anchor (see Figure 1) to keep the bow into the wind.

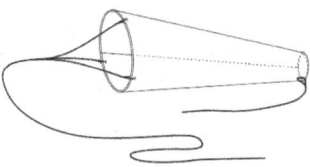

Figure 1: Sea Anchor or Drogue

Most sailboats will remain afloat even in the worst storms but the people inside get battered pretty well if the bow is not held into the wind. Powerboats are more vulnerable to heavy seas. The sea anchor, drift anchor or drogue (there are other names), can be a safety device or it can be used for controlled drifting for diving or fishing.

Before using any device under duress, you need to practice using it on a nice day. Otherwise you will make mistakes under panic circumstances.

Size of the drogue, length of the rode and inclusion of a trip line should be thought out before you try to use it. Use the following recommendations:

- The size is determined by the manufacturer.
- Use between 50 and 150 ft of anchor rode attached to the drogue.
- Be sure to include a trip line attached to the tip so you will be able to reel it in backwards when necessary.
- Attach a float with a length of line (around 1 meter) between the float and the tip of the drogue. This will keep it from sinking if the winds die down and make it easier to recover.

The trip line should float and doesn't need to be super strong. Quarter inch Polypropylene line is fine. Be sure to pay out more trip line than anchor rode so there is no stress on the trip line. Since polypropylene is affected by the sun, be sure it is stored away from the sun or protected in a suitable bag.

Know Where You Are and How to Get Where You Are Going

It does a Captain no good to have a flawless vessel with no idea where he or she is. It also does the Captain no good to have electronic charts with a GPS that fails while the boat is in heavy seas. This is an area that requires redundancy. The Captain should always have a compass and a chart and know where the boat is on the chart. A GPS with built-in, up-to-date charts will make life a lot easier for the skipper, but neither the Captain nor the passengers should not get too comfortable with the fallible electronic wizardry. The Captain should always have paper charts and compass as a backup, and be prepared to use them as part of his or her navigational plan. With today's technology, it is too easy to substitute point-and-click electronic marvels for navigational mastery. While a Captain should feel free to use them, he or she should also have good old-fashioned backup compass and charts.

Prevent Fire

Fiberglass and wooden boats burn well. Even steel vessels have plenty of fuel on board to cause a fire large enough to cripple or sink it. Keep the fire from starting in the first place.

Fires start on board due to DC and AC short circuits, poor AC and DC connections, engine voltage regulator failures, electric heaters, overheating engines, and fuel leaks. Electric coffee pots and other appliances are also potential fire risks. Most of these are due to poor maintenance.

Corroded electrical terminals create resistance, which creates heat, which causes fires and other failures. There is no excuse for corrosion in electronic terminals. The marine environment is harsh due to salt water and high humidity, but dielectric grease and regular inspections can prevent disaster. Marine maintenance literature does not talk about this enough.

Dielectric grease is simple and inexpensive to use. It keeps moisture away from the electrical connection so it won't corrode. The "dielectric" part means it does not conduct electricity and therefore will not interfere with the proper control of electricity. The Captain could coat any part of any electric or electronic connection and the device would still work fine. He or she will need to keep the substance away from moving parts and heat sinks, however, as it might interfere.

Short circuits occur when a wire comes loose or the insulation is damaged so that it touches something that completes an unwanted circuit. In all cases there should be a fuse that will immediately blow and reduce the danger. The Captain should make sure this is always the case. Fuses should be located as near to the source of electricity as possible but still be accessible. If no fuse exists to stop the flow of electricity, then heat is generated and has the potential to cause a fire.

If a fire does occur, the U.S. Coast Guard requires all boats to have fire extinguisher capability onboard, at a minimum. In all cases the Captain should really have additional and redundant fire extinguishing capabilities, though he or she clearly needs to meet the Coast Guard regulation.

The bottom line is the Captain of the boat needs to be aware of everything about the vessel and use that awareness to keep people and property safe from harm. This book will help a Captain determine some of the things to be aware of and what to do about different situations. The book will specifically deal with reliability issues a Captain can and should do something about.

Vessel Configuration and Maintenance

The configuration and the condition of the vessel plays a large part in keeping everyone safe. According to the U.S. Coast Guard, hundreds of people die each year as a result of boating accidents [18]. Some of these accidents result from poor operation and others result from poor configuration and maintenance.

Included in the configuration of the boat is the complete set of safety equipment required by the U.S. Coast Guard. There are plenty of places to get this information so we will not discuss the details here. We do, however, recommend the Captain obtains a USCG Auxiliary Courtesy Marine Examination of the boat. Canada has a similar examination. It is available in most areas and is well worth the effort for the Captain to have another set of experienced eyes on his or her vessel. The regulations are detailed just to make sure it gets done.

The Captain should also read a copy of *Chapman Piloting Seamanship and Boat Handling*. The Captain is well advised to obtain as much information as he or she can to be aware of his or her boat.

Alcohol Use While Operating a Boat

The simplest thing a Captain can do to increase the probability of a serious accent is to operate his or her vessel under the influence of alcohol or other mind-altering drug.

While the Coast Guard and state boating law authorities suspect alcohol use to be a major factor in the high number of recreational boating fatalities (about 600 to 800 a year), creditable national statistics are not available[22].

Safety Board studies estimate at least 37% of the operators involved in fatal accidents were known to have or were presumed to have consumed alcohol before their accidents occurred. Information reported to the USCG in 2003 indicates that approximately 32% of all boating fatalities were alcohol related[23].

Crew Responsibilities

Occupants of any boat must understand and give the skipper the authority he or she needs to keep the vessel safe. If the skipper yells, "Jump!" the passengers and crew should jump. Whether the Captain is planning a short trip or a long one, he or she should review the safety features of the boat with his or her passengers. The Captain should tell them where the dangerous areas on the boat are, what to touch and what not to touch. If the Captain needs the passengers to help him or her dock, then the Captain should let them know what they need to do well before they need to do it.

Have you ever watched a distressed husband and wife team coming into the dock? The Captain husband is barking out orders to his wife, who is clueless as to what he wants. She is doing the best she can but the real problem is the Captain didn't let her know what he wanted her to do. I have done this myself on many occasions. This can be a major source of entertainment on a windy day.

The funniest instance I've ever seen of this is the time I saw a husband tell his wife to jump onto the dock to hold the boat with no line in her hand. She dutifully jumped, then tried to hold onto the boat railing while the wind took it away. She wasn't strong enough to hold the boat and had no line to wrap around a cleat, so she hung on right into the water. To this day, I can still see her hanging from the railing while everyone on shore was laughing. This is not the way to improve relationships.

Obviously, the goal of having a recreational boat is to enjoy it, but since the skipper is ultimately responsible for the boat, he or she should readily take control. If this means barking out orders, so be it. If you want to be a Captain with a crew, you should be nice, think ahead, and communicate the thinking to your crew before someone gets wet.

Chapter 3: Reliability Analysis

When a U.S. Navy vessel leaves port, the Captain knows he or she will be able to return to port. This confidence comes from a combination of the design of the ship, the supportability plan, operational procedures, and the training of the crew. If the owner of the *Questar* had thought about what could go wrong, he could have taken measures to make his boat more reliable and save his life.

One surefire way for a boat owner to make his or her boat more reliable is to analyze the boat and the systems on it, and then make informed choices about adding or replacing components that would best increase reliability. While performing the analysis, the owner should make plans and examine his or her boat for potential failures. There is never a 100% guarantee of anything, but an owner can increase the likelihood of achieving his or her goals manyfold by analyzing, creating a plan, and implementing the changes he or she identifies. In this way, the owner can make sure the Captain, crew, and passengers are safe except for extreme freaks of nature where only God can save everyone onboard.

Reliability modeling and prediction employs objective methods to determine the probability that a particular device will fulfill its intended mission. NASA and the U.S. military use reliability modeling extensively when designing machines that must last under harsh conditions or incur catastrophic results. Spacecraft, missiles, aircraft, and ships are examples of vessels that can cause loss of life or mission failure if critical components break down. It takes teams of engineers just to design one of these vessels. Designers know exactly what the probability of failure is for their designs. During the design process, they use objective reliability estimation to determine the best configuration. They also know how to analyze and trade off important design criteria.

When making design decisions, engineers make trade-offs between costs, weight, and reliability. There is rarely a cost-effective, 99.99% reliable solution. They use rigorous analyses in order to validate the designs.

The magnitude of a reliable design is far beyond the scope of most boat owners, though their situation is a little different. They can get away with less rigorous methods, but they still need an analysis that will help get their vessels into the most reliable condition.

To compete in the recreational boat market, boat designers accept the possibility of catastrophic failure in their leisure boat designs. Many components in the power train, for example, can fail and leave everyone onboard stranded. Conventional wisdom says to just get a tow home and take the boat to the local mechanic. This process is fine for the fair weather local boater but not for a boat cruising far away from homeport or far away from land. A better approach is for the designer to ensure the boat will make it to its destination and back again so that a tow would not be necessary. Designers can dramatically increase this probability through proper reliability analysis, equipment configuration, and planning.

Some critical components are reliable and seldom fail, some components will let an owner know how long he or she has before they totally fail and leave those onboard stranded, and some components will fail without warning. Boat owners need to know which are reliable, which are not, and what the consequences of failure would be for every component on his or her boat. Only then can an owner make informed decisions about how to upgrade reliability. This book will teach boat owners how to analyze their boats and figure out the best approach to reliability.

This book addresses three basic areas:
- How to analyze the reliability of a vessel
- How to increase the reliability of a system by proper application of redundancy and monitoring

- How to increase the probability of success by proper configuration, planning, supply, and operation

If you own a boat, keep these basic issues in mind as you analyze the reliability of your boat.

Reliability Prediction

Reliability prediction is a best estimate of the reliability of a particular machine, system, or component within certain limitations. Engineers use this method to determine the best design and proper maintenance activities. A proper reliability model will produce a probability estimate. Evaluation of different equipment configurations use probability estimates to validate a particular design.

Reliability engineering defines mean time between failures (MTBF) and failure rate, though the two terms are really the same thing. Failure rate is the reciprocal of MTBF. In other words 1/MTBF = failure rate. A failure rate of .001 means an engineer can expect .001 failures every hour. The reciprocal of that is the MTBF of 1000, which means the engineer can expect one failure every 1000 hours. So failure rate and MTBF mean the same thing; they're just expressed in different terms.

Not all components take part in the reliability analysis, only those components that are required to perform the mission goal do. These are called "critical components." Boat owners need to identify their critical components as they perform reliability planning.

Important terms:

- Critical component is a component that performs a critical function, one that is required to achieve a goal.
- Failure rate is how many failures can an owner expect in an hour. Our example is .001 failures per hour.
- Mean Time Between Failure (MTBF) indicates how often boat owners can expect a failure. Our example is 1/.001 = 1000 or 1 failure every 1000 hours.

Bathtub Curve

The reliability of most individual components falls on "the bathtub curve" (see Figure 2) which shows the expected reliability of a component throughout its life. At the beginning and end of a life cycle, the expected failure rate is high. These high failure rates are for short time periods of unknown duration. On the other hand, the middle of the component life cycle enjoys a low expected failure rate. This is good because it means the component spends most of its time in the middle part of the bathtub curve.

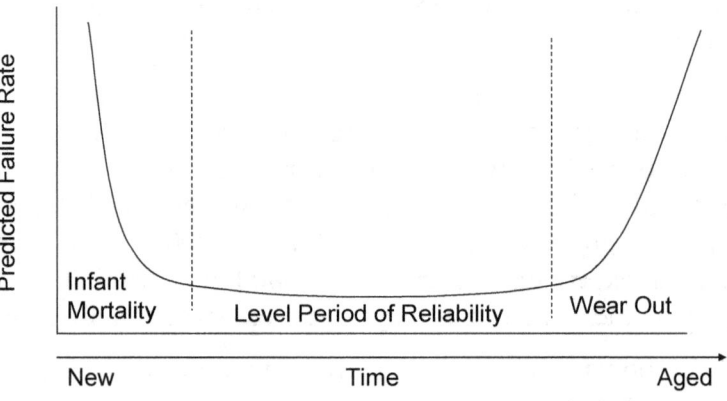

Figure 2: Bathtub Curve

Failures in the early part of the life cycle are called infant mortality failures. These are due to imperfect manufacturing. There might be a loose bolt, a forgotten part, or an invisible crack in a casting. Any number of things can go wrong and slip through the inspection process. If you bought a new American automobile in the 1970s, you were almost guaranteed in the first months of ownership to bring your car back to the dealer for multiple infant mortality failures. If you were lucky, you did not get stuck on the road, after dark, in the rain, and need a tow.

During 1970s and 1980s, the Japanese imported more and more cars to the United States. The quality of the Japanese cars was so good that it caused U.S car manufacturers to increase the quality of their automobiles. Today, your car might still have an infant mortality failure, but it's not as likely.

The bottom line is that whenever you install a new critical component in your boat, always remember the bathtub curve. Give your new component a chance to prove itself in fair circumstances. In other words, do not install a new fuel pump and then immediately cruise across the Atlantic. Test the component close to shore on a few nice days before fully relying on it.

The first Sailboat race around the world included an example of infancy failure. In 1968, Donald Crowhurst was one of nine contestants in a race to become the first person to circumnavigate the world; single handed and non-stop. Crowhurst was the least experienced and the least prepared. In fact his yacht was experimental and the first time he sailed it was the start of the race. It is an interesting story but it ends in tragedy when early on in the race his boat is disabled due to infancy mortality of the boat and all of its systems.

Abby Sunderland, a teenager from southern California, attempted to sail around the world by herself. It seems she had enough experience, backing and training. The problem with Abby's voyage is that she had too much backing. They built her a special boat, gave her special state of the art equipment and infinite support. She ended up having more problems from her new equipment that hadn't been fully tested. The boat was abandoned somewhere in the Indian Ocean. She survived due to multiple EPIRBs (Emergency Position Indicating Radio Beacon) that went off after the boat was dismasted. Again, not fully tried and tested.

Laura Dekker on the other hand was successful shortly after Suderland's failure. Dekker had no special boat or state of the art equipment.

Maybe it was not the equipment that made the difference but you know now that all of your equipment needs to be tried and tested beyond the infant mortality stage before relying on it for your life.

At the end of a component's life cycle comes another period of high probability of failure because of the component wearing out. When this happens, you will need to have a plan of action. Use one of the methods outlined in this book to deal with any component failure.

The middle or main part of the life cycle is the longest period on the bathtub curve. During the middle or main part of the curve, the failure rate is relatively low and constant. The component can still fail at any time during this period but with the same probability, and a much lower probability than at the beginning and end of the component life cycle. The component is just as likely to fail at the beginning as at the end of the main part of the curve. I will use the bathtub curve to explain why you need to prove and test your components before completely relying on them.

Remember the bathtub curve when installing new critical components required for proper operation. For example, do not set out across the ocean with a brand-new fuel pump until you run the pump for a while or unless you carry a spare.

Redundancy
The U.S. military defines redundancy in MIL-STD-721 as follows:

- Redundancy – The existence of more than one means for accomplishing a given function. Each means of accomplishing the function need not necessarily be identical.
- Active Redundancy – A redundancy wherein all redundant items are operating simultaneously.
- Standby Redundancy – A redundancy wherein an alternative means of performing the function is not operating until it is activated upon failure of the primary means of performing the function.

Active redundancy is when multiple components are running all the time but if one fails the boat is still operational while the failed component is fixed. The performance might be degraded but the function is feasible. An example would be having two engines. If one engine fails, it is still possible to control the boat and get back to port at a degraded speed and with less maneuverability. This type of configuration is about twice as reliable as components in series.

With standby redundancy, only one component operates at a time. A "standby" component is present just in case another component fails. One example is having an electric fuel pump installed and ready to be activated when the main fuel pump fails. Standby redundancy is the most reliable configuration because it is 99% reliable after the redundant components pass into the middle part of the bathtub reliability curve. If a component has never been used, its reliability is low due to infant mortality.

It is important to verify all standby redundant components so that they move beyond the early part of the bathtub curve. In the case of the redundant fuel pump, using it from time to time would provide verification that the pump is viable.

Reliability Modeling

Modeling is the way to determine the reliability of any given system. In military systems, the DOD requires a system to meet a certain reliability figure, which is modeled using a mathematical representation of the system reliability and a certain availability. If, for example, the requirement for a particular system is "99% available for operation," that means the system must be available for use 99% of the time. If a critical component does fail, it must be able to be repaired in time to meet the requirement.

Consider a bicycle. Let's say the tires have a MTBF of 99 hours and it takes an average of one hour to fix a tire. That means the owner of the bike will have to spend 1 of every 100 hours fixing a tire. In a formula form:

$$\text{Availability} = \text{MTBF}/(\text{MTBF} + \text{repair time})$$

So, in the bicycle example, the availability would be 99/99+1 = 99.9%.

This approach is great for military systems that have a team of engineers to determine all the necessary numbers and people trained to fix whatever goes wrong. For non-military applications, we need an approach that's less rigorous but still useful for predicting how available a boat will be.

In the next section, therefore, we will define a new type of reliability model that will allow the boat owner or maintainer to determine how to best configure, supply, and plan for reliable boating. If you're a boat owner, producing this type of reliability model for your boat is a worthwhile endeavor if you are interested in optimizing the reliability of your boat. You will need to base your analysis on cost, skill, and usage. Before getting into the details, however, let's examine some of the details from the military reliability model.

Reliability Calculations

Note: Do not spend too much time mastering these formulas. They are here for completeness. We'll introduce a simpler method later in this chapter. You might want to skip the section on Failure Mode Risk Analysis if you don't care about the details of reliability analysis.

Mean Time Between Failure (MTBF)

Failure rate (FR) – Reciprocal of MTBF or FR = 1/MTBF

If we know the failure rate, then we can calculate the probability the component will fail over a given time period.

Probability for failure = e ^(time * (-FR))

Where:

time is the amount of time
FR is the failure rate
e is the natural log or ~2.718281828…

Reliability (Probability of Success)

Reliability is the probability an item can perform its intended function for a specified interval under stated conditions [MIL-STD- 271].

Reliability then is a probability. Now we need to calculate the probability based on the failure rate.

R(t) = e $^{-fr * t}$

where

R(t) is the reliability at time **t**, or the probability that a given component, or system of components, will survive at time **t**.

e is the base of the natural logarithms or 2.718281828…

fr is the failure rate over the time period. Remember failure rate is the reciprocal of MTBF.

t is time at the point we are calculating.

As an example, Figure 3 is a graph of a component that has a MTBF of 1000 hours. Use the chart to get an idea of the reliability of any particular component on your boat. Just change the time scale. If, for example, you are considering a very reliable component that has, say, a MTBF of 10000 hours, simply multiple the time scale by 10.

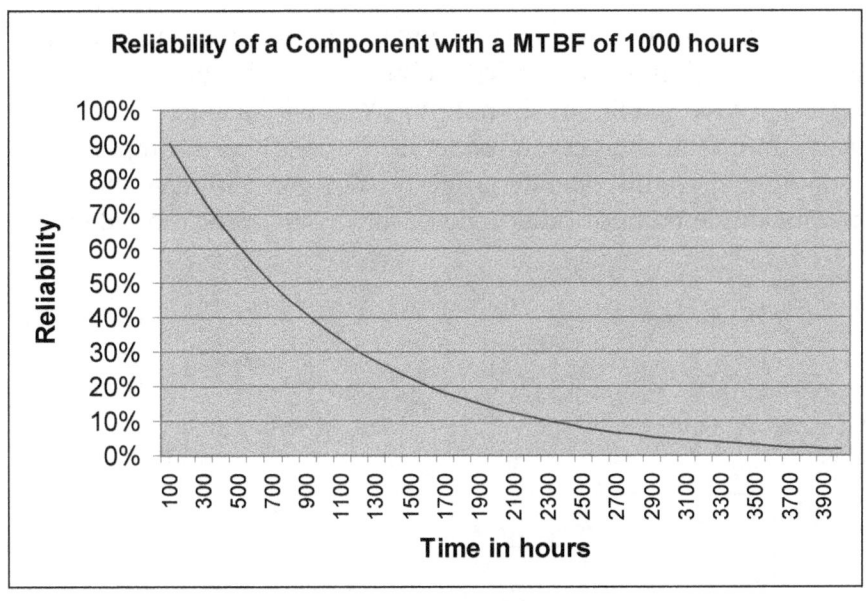

Figure 3: Reliability Curve

You can combine the reliability formula in Figure 3 in different ways to accurately assess the reliability of a whole system as long as you know the failure rate of each component and how the components are assembled to satisfy a particular goal. While a system relying on a single component will have a certain reliability, it will have a much better reliability and a better chance of success if it has 10 components but only needs one.

Component "Series" Reliability

Components in "series" are all required for any mission to be successful. If any one component in a series configuration fails, the entire system fails. If, for example, one of the tires on your car fails and you have no spare, you cannot drive the car.

Figure 4 is an example of a series components diagram. This is only a basic illustration and does not include all the necessary components of an engine. The figure is just an example to show that both a fuel pump and a carburetor (among other components) are needed for an engine to run because the fuel pump is needed to get the fuel to the carburetor.

You will also need a cooling subsystem with a circulating pump and a raw water pump. You will also need an ignition coil because if you do not have a spark, your engine will not run. You will also need a starter motor and a means to charge your battery. If any of these components fails, your engine will not operate properly. You can eliminate the problem of a single point of failure, however, by applying redundancy.

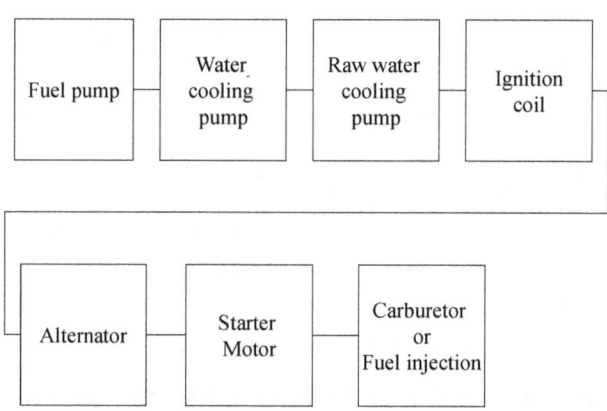

Figure 4: Series Model

Multiple Component Reliability (Parallel)

The parallel model is a basic model used for multiple components that are not all needed, where only a subset is required for operation. You might have 2 fuel pumps, but only need one, for example. Figure 5 is an example of a parallel reliability model. The parallel mode represents redundancy. This is the best way to increase the reliability of a system.

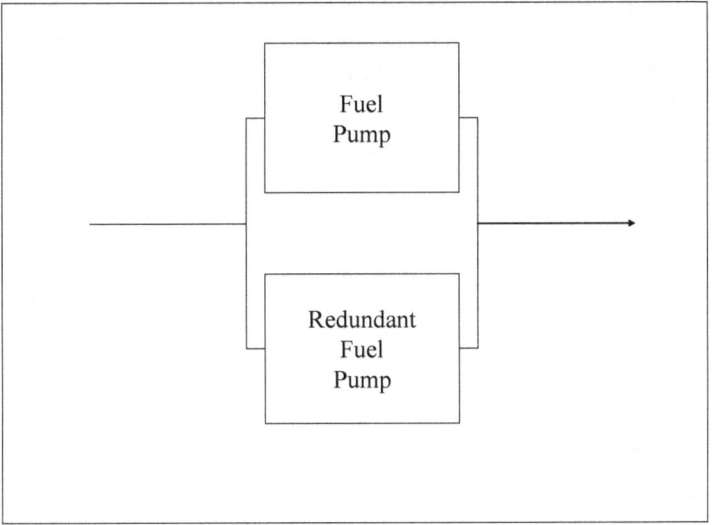

Figure 5: Parallel Redundant Components

Multiple Component Reliability (Series/Parallel)

In some cases, you will have components that are both in series and parallel, such as double wheels on a single axle where one of the two wheels on each end of the axel is required for successful operation. Figure 6 depicts the combination of the series and parallel model and shows 3 sets of redundant "parallel" components that are all required in a "series" model.

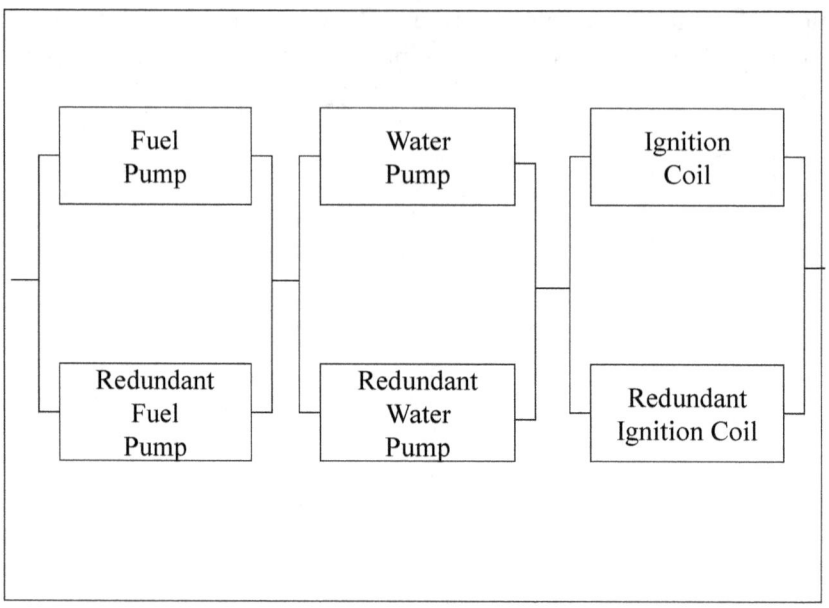

Figure 6: Series/Parallel Model

In a series model, the reliability of multiple single components can be combined. The probability of success for each component in the system is multiplied to give the combined probability of success.

If, for example, components A, B, C, & D have a probability of success of P(A), P(B), P(C), & P(D), their combined probability of success PF would be:

$$PF = P(A) * P(B) * P(C) * P(D)$$

(Multiple Components Probability of Success)

Multiple Redundant Component Reliability

The probability of success for multiple active redundant components is calculated as follows: For 2 components "A" with a probability of success of P(A), assuming only one of them is needed for a particular job, their combined probability of success would be:

$$PF = 2 * P(A) - P(A)^2$$

(Active Redundancy Probability of Success)

Any time redundancy is used, reliability increases. Standby redundancy provides much greater short-term reliability, however. Since the standby component is new, reliability engineers give it a 100% reliability for near-term operations. This clearly is the best strategy for getting back to homeport. Note: As discussed, the bathtub curve predicts a high failure rate for new components. For this reason redundant components should be designed so they can be operated at will. This allows both designers and owners alike to make sure the redundant components work properly and force them beyond the infant mortality part of the "bathtub" reliability curve.

If multiple components are configured in a standby redundant situation, the probability of failure can be calculated. For 2 components, "A" with a probability of failure of P(A) and a near-term probability of operability of NTP(A) = 99.9%, the probability of success would be:

$$PF = P(A) + NTP(A) - P(A) * NTP(A)$$

(Probability of success for standby redundant components)

Table 2 shows an example of the reliability for multiple components configured in each of the 3 ways: series, active redundant, and standby redundant. Given the stated probabilities, the table shows a single component would provide 50% reliability, 2 of the same required components would provide 25%, and two of the same components where only one was needed would provide 75%. If a standby active component was available, however, a 99.995% reliability would be achieved. Standby redundancy is clearly a major advantage over the others.

Table 2: Probability of Success for Various Components

Reliability parameters	
P(A)	50%
P(B)	50%
NTP(A)	99.99%
Combined reliability	
Single component	50%
Two components in series	25%
Two components in Active redundancy	75%
One component in Standby redundancy	99.995%

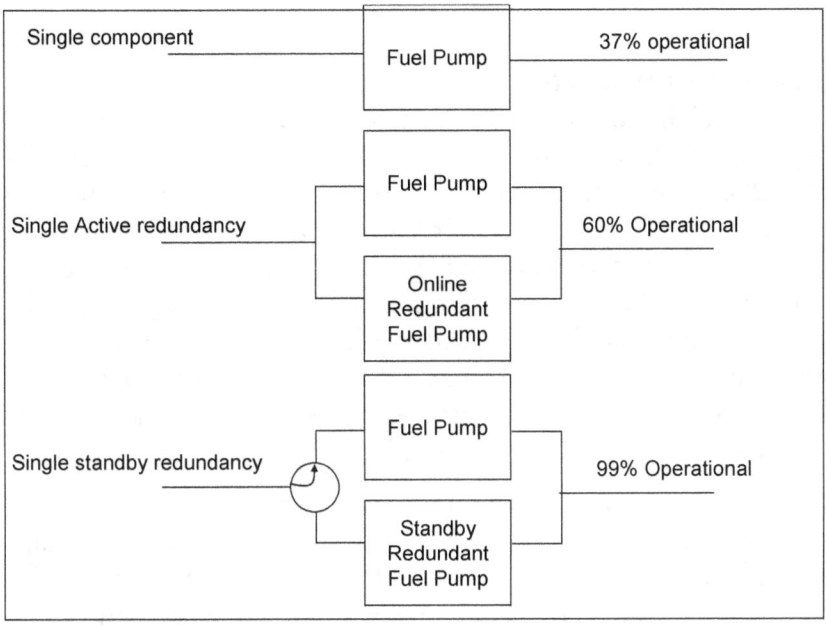

Figure 7: Operational Redundancy

Based on an exponential distribution, what are the chances a certain item will fail in a certain amount of time? Figure 7 shows an example of the three reliability configurations: series, parallel, and stand-by redundancy. Let's say our fuel pump has a Mean Time Between Failure (MTBF) of 2000 hours. By applying the exponential distribution we determine there is only a 37% chance the component will still be operating in 2000 hours. If we add a redundant component, we experience a 60% chance that the subsystem will still be operational. If we add a standby redundant component, however, we will have a 99% chance of still having the necessary functionality. Clearly standby redundancy is the key to our mission success.

As you go through the process of applying standby redundancy, remember the bathtub curve. If you never use a standby component until you need it, you will be operating in the initial part of the bathtub curve that is not reliable due to manufacturing defects. Always test out your standby redundant components to provide confidence that the redundant component is working and is beyond the infant mortality part of the bathtub curve.

Propulsion Reliability

One of the most important systems on your boat is the propulsion system, which consists of several components modeled in series. The largest and least reliable components group is the engine. While boat engines were designed to be used in harsh sea environments, they are normally far less than 99.9% reliable. Manufacturers assume the Captain will likely have failures on board, but that he or she will get a tow back to port and have the engine serviced at a local marina. This is not the best approach, however, for those on a long voyage or in rough weather. A better approach would be to increase the reliability of the propulsion plant so everyone onboard can stay safe.

Now let's determine the failure rate of a typical single inboard engine. The first thing to do is to identify the critical components and groups of components, then determine how reliable the components are. We then use probability formulas to calculate how reliable the configuration is. This is called modeling. We can try different configurations in order to optimize the critical reliability based on cost weight and other constraints. As we will see, it is possible to almost guarantee a 99.9% probability of mission success, but that comes at a price.

Engine

Table 3 depicts a short list of engine components with sample failure data. If we combine these engine components in the reliability calculation, we see that we are likely to have a successful 3-hour cruise (see Figure 8). As the season goes on and the hours mount up, however, the probability of success becomes a 50-50 proposition after about 200 hours of operation. Obviously, if we just keep running our engine without maintenance, eventually we will have a failure.

Some of the failures we have allow us to operate until we get back to shore and get the problem fixed, but not always. It is, therefore, important that we address the problems that might happen and increase our probability of success. If a redundant engine is included, the reliability increases quite a bit in the 20- to 700-hour range. Continuing the logic; if certain standby redundant components are added, the reliability for the system increases in the 250+ hours. Now it is up to the owner of the boat to determine what the best situation is for maximizing his or her vessel's reliability.

Table 3: Typical Single-Engine Components

Component	Reliability Notes	MTBF	Failure Rate
Engine long-block – includes pistons, crankshaft, valve train, associated bearings, etc.	Very reliable until wear-out period. There is generally advanced warning when something in the engine block fails.	2000	.002
Carburetor/fuel injection	Usually gives advanced warning. Carburetor is essential in proper starting and running. Usually gives advanced warning before catastrophic failure.	1500	.0015
Fuel pump	Fuel pumps can fail and leave you stranded.	1000	.001
Cooling circulating pump	These can fail and ruin the rest of your engine. You need to monitor flow and temperature here.	500	.0005
Alternator	Alternators bearings fail, leaving you without charging capability. Also, it will keep the fan belt from moving and, therefore, you will not have cooling re-circulation or power steering.	800	.0008
Battery	Batteries are in a different category than other components. If they are allowed to drain, they can	-	

	leave you stranded. They also lose the ability to recharge when frequently discharged. Otherwise they are quite reliable.		
Raw water-cooling pump	This is the pump that brings cooling water either into the heat exchanger or directly into the engine. In either case a failure here can cause catastrophic loss of mobility and perhaps cause major damage to your engine.	200	.02

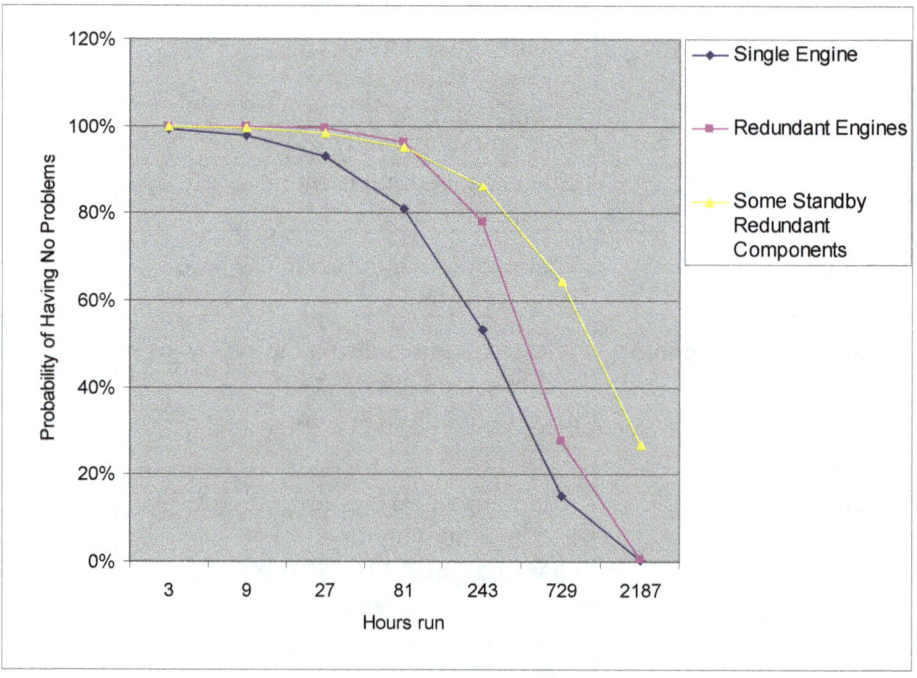

Figure 8: Probability of NO Failure

Chapter 4: A Systems Approach to a Reliable Boat

Hundreds of individual parts on a boat can fail, leaving everyone onboard stranded. The bathtub curve only applies to fairly simple mechanisms. More complicated systems fail randomly. With random failures no maintenance procedures or overhaul schedule will provide known reliability. The best we can do is predict a failure and plan contingencies far enough ahead of time to fix the problem in time to minimize its impact.

There are several approaches a boat owner can take to determine if his or her boat is reliable enough. The first question the owner must answer is, "How am I going to use my boat?" followed by other questions such as, "What systems do I rely on?" "What are their functions?" "How do they fail?" and "What are the consequences of failure?" Some of the failures an owner defines will probably never happen, while some might happen without causing significant impact to the boat's intended use. Resources need to be applied to potential failures that will have a significant impact on the operation of the boat and the safety of everyone onboard if they do occur.

The general approach is to:

- Define the systems and subsystems on the boat.
- Define how they can fail (failure mode).
- Define the consequences of failure.
- Determine the likelihood of failure modes.

- Define contingency plans. Determine how to fix the problem if a failure mode occurs.
- Prioritize contingencies based on both the likelihood and consequence of failure.
- Determine how to best predict a failure with a maximum warning time.
- Plan for contingencies based on the prioritization scheme. Apply judgment based on experience and knowledge.

The next sections provide some background of failure mode analysis and risk management, followed by an outline and an example of a combined approach.

The FMEA Process – Identifying Problems

One tool used to determine reliability for any system or sets of systems is the Failure Modes and Effects Analysis (FMEA), developed by the Society of Automobile Engineers' (SAE) reliability engineers. Some engineers get hung up on the definition of "failure" vs. that of "fault," however, and call the process Fault Hazard Analysis. Whatever you call it, the FMEA allows engineers to analyze the effects caused by system-element failures, and helps them determine how vulnerable a system is to the types of failures that might be experienced. The FMEA can be used to determine the best area to put extra redundancy and reliability into factories, spaceships, boats, or anything else that uses a complex set of components that work together as a system.

There is not a firm process for FMEA that everyone uses. Instead, different companies use different process steps to define FEMA. Following is a modified FEMA process similar to the one used by the Ford Motor Company.

Identity the Potential Problems

List the equipment. This includes all the equipment and components on your boat. Here you can break the system down into system, subsystems, assemblies, and subassemblies. We have provided an analysis and a breakdown in the accompanying spreadsheet. You may modify it or perform your own.
(http://TheReliableBoat.com/ExtraStuff)

Identify the functions served by the identified equipment.

Identify potential failure modes of the identified equipment. In other words, what can happen to a component that might cause it to fail? Some examples might be old age, poor maintenance, or excessive moisture.

List the potential effects of the failure of the component.

Define the severity rating or consequence of a component failure (see Table 4).

Define potential failure mechanisms. Why did the mechanisms fail? What is the root cause of the failure?

Assign an occurrence rating to each failure mechanism. This is the Mean Time Between Failures.

Identify the Potential Solutions

Identify predictive monitoring techniques. Advanced monitoring reduces the impact of a failure by providing a warning in advance of the actual failure. List the various techniques by which each failure might be detected.

Assign a detection rating to each failure mode/mechanism. How well can we detect the problem? Good? Fair? Poor?

Assign a likelihood to each fault, calculate a risk-factor number (RF), and apply thresholds to determine the risk level of each fault type. This is used to help determine which faults should be dealt with first.

Identify a recommended action for each fault type. This is any action you take to reduce the probability of the failure or reduce the consequence. A filter, for example, might have a 40% chance it will become clogged. If you carry a spare, however, you will reduce the likelihood of that happing to <10%.

Based on the analysis, determine which of the mechanisms you will want to address.

While FMEA is an excellent tool for determining the reliability of a system made up of many components, it takes specialized training and hard-to-find data to complete a meaningful analysis. Moreover, the results are not produced in the language of the domain and are, therefore, hard for the untrained to understand.

So while FMEA is useful for highly trained engineers with a staff of maintenance personnel, the average boat owner needs a better way to analyze the reliability of his or her boat.

Risk Management - Risk of Failure

Risk management is a project management technique that tries to see forward in time to determine what could happen to prevent a project from meeting its goals. Risk management does not require highly specialized and difficult training, so many different project management teams, from industry to the military, use it to watch and manage risks as a project progresses.

Risk management identifies and prioritizes goals and risks, and then plans for mitigating the risks over the life of the program. It also prioritizes risks by assigning a "risk factor" to each risk, thereby allowing a management team to work on the largest risks first. If a risk is determined too risky, mitigation procedures can be developed to reduce the probability that the risk will happen or reduce the consequence or the likelihood of the risk happening.

First, a management team defines the likelihood and consequence of each risk. The likelihood defines how likely the risk is to occur. This is a judgment call and is defined in normal language terms, for example, "highly likely" or "not likely."

The consequence denotes how the risk will affect the project's objectives if the risk ever occurs. The consequence is also defined in the language of the domain. "Loss of mobility," "Fire," and "Flood," for example, are potential consequences to the boat owner.

A number is assigned to each likelihood and consequence type. The risk factor (RF) can then be calculated based on these assignments. The RF provides a pseudo-objective means of assessing the relative risk for a particular fault. The results are used to evaluate relative risks regarding the system under analysis. It is based on the understanding and objectives of the evaluator. The risk factor calculation prioritizes risk to address the highest potential risks first.

Table 5 depicts a sample set of likelihood values with their relative meanings. A likelihood of remote possibility, for example, would get a 0.1 according to the table. In order to properly assign values, a time frame of reference is needed to tie the values to. The likelihood the bilges pump system will fail in the next three hours, for example, is "remote." It is highly likely, however, that the same system will fail sometime during the next 5 years. The timeframe, for example, can be one summer, the lifetime of a boat, or 10 years. Use the same timeframe for all likelihood decisions.

The other factor we must determine is the consequence if a particular fault occurs. Table 4 defines a set of criteria for the consequences. Your consequences should be the worst possible things that could happen if a fault occurs. If your boat's fuel filter gets clogged, for example, in reality you could still operate the boat in a degraded manner, but the worst that could happen is your engine could quit and your boat would lose mobility.

Table 5 assigns a numerical value to a particular fault. If you asked, for example, "How likely is it that a bilge pump will fail in the next 10 years?" the answer might be "highly likely," which you might assign a numeric value of 0.7. This assessment system is an ongoing process that includes periodic reviews and updates of the values.

Be sure to assign each consequence as separate entries. If, for example, you listed "flooding and/or sinking" as your consequence, these are really two different risk entries. It might be "highly likely" that something in your boat will fail that will cause it to flood, but "less likely" that you will sink. So you would say:

- It is highly likely that we will flood as a result of a bilge pump failure sometime in the next 10 years.
- It is unlikely that we will sink as a result of a bilge pump failure sometime in the next 10 years.

Table 4: Consequence of a Fault

.1	Loss of redundancy
.3	Degradation of operation
.5	Loss of capability
.7	Loss of mobility
.9	Loss of life

Table 5: Likelihood of a Fault

%	Numerical	Notional
.1	0 – 20%	Remote
.3	21 – 40%	Unlikely
.5	41 – 60%	Likely
.7	61 – 80%	Highly Likely
.9	81 – 100%	Near Certainty

Risk Factor Calculation (places more emphasis on consequence and less on likelihood):

$$RF = 1-(1-C)^L$$

Alternate Risk Factor Calculation (treats likelihood and consequence the same)

$$RF = .5 *(C+L)$$

Where

C is the Consequence

L is the Likelihood
A Risk Level (RL) is then assigned based on the Risk Factor as follows:

Risk Level is
Low if RF < .2
Medium if 0.4 > RF >= 0.2
High if RF >= 0.4

Risk level colors can be assigned as follows:
Red = High
Yellow = Medium (Moderate)
Green = Low

In Figure 9 each risk is in one of the colored squares.

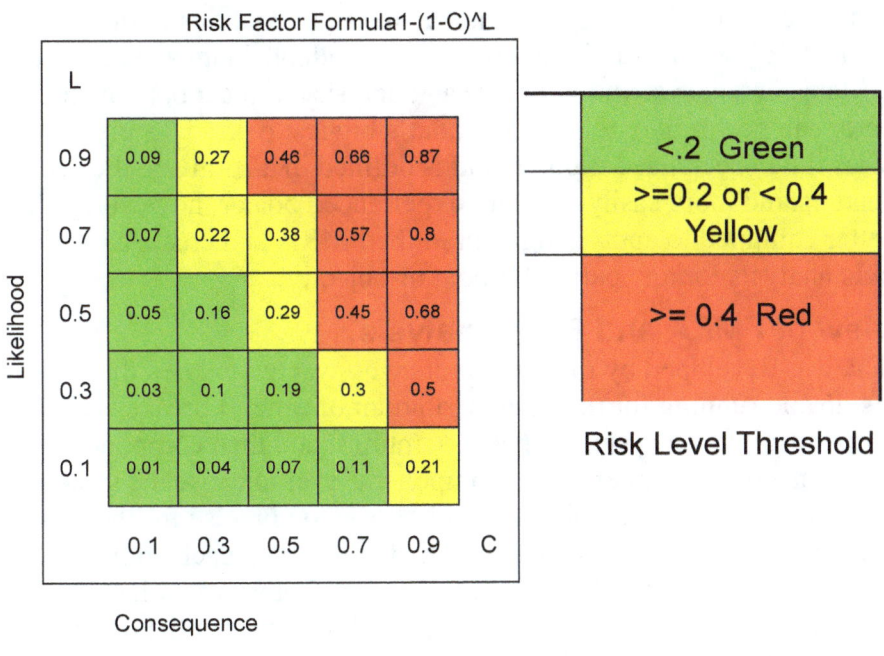

Figure 9: Risk Factor Calculation

Don't get too hung up on exact values or precise meanings of "likelihood," "consequence," and "risk factor." Remember this is a pseudo-objective approach to analyzing the reliability of your boat that allows you to determine the greatest risks to your objectives so you can properly apply resources. Keep applying common sense. It should point you to the systems and components that need to be addressed and the relative priority in which each should be addressed.

Even though risk analysis is an excellent, easy-to-understand tool for identifying, quantifying, and managing risk, it does not provide the rigor needed for each component to get the attention required for near perfect reliability.

Risks to a Captain's objectives are too nebulous and numerous for a reliability analysis, however. We still need another easy approach, therefore, to analyze a boat's reliability.

Failure Mode Risk Analysis (FMRA)

FMRA is an analysis that determines the risk a particular system cannot meet its intended objectives. It combines the rigor of the previously defined FMEA process and the more understandable language of the Risk Management system to achieve an analysis a typical boat owner or operator can perform to determine a boat's biggest risks. This method requires little specialized training and is defined in a language the user can understand more easily. A more experienced boater, however, will be better equipped to apply judgment to the FMRA and create a more reliable analysis for any particular boat or objective.

Review of FMEA and Risk Analysis

FMEA was developed by manufacturers who wanted to keep their plants up and running for the optimal amount of time. It breaks each system down into subsystems, then assemblies, and then components to analyze what could happen at the component level to cause the system to fail to achieve its intended objective. FMEA is too precise for the average person and requires hard-to-find details about each component. The results of a proper FMEA are excellent for factories that have a team of engineers and maintenance personnel to carry out the process because it provides them with an objective assessment of how reliable and available their equipment is.

Risk Analysis uses language that is clear to everyone who understands the domain. Risk analysis can use words like, "remote," "unlikely," "likely," "highly likely," or "near certainty," for example, to define the probability of a risk happening. It can also use words like "loss of redundancy," "degraded operation," "loss of capability," "loss of mobility," and "loss of life" to define the consequence of a risk, and assigns numbers and calculations to those words to determine the relative magnitude of each risk. The results are understandable to anyone who can read.

Both these techniques are good examples of how large teams of engineers and managers handle their day-to-day work. They both require more skill than the average person would like to develop, however, but if we combine them into a single technique and develop an analysis for a particular class of machinery, such as "boats," we have an easier-to-use, but still meaningful, analysis, the objective of which is to apply resources to maximize the reliability of a particular boat for a particular mission.

Following are the steps of the FMRA process:

Identify Potential Problems (Risks)
- List the critical equipment ordered by systems and subsystems.
- Identify failure modes of each piece of critical equipment. How can each critical component fail?
- List the potential effects of each failure mode. This includes the direct effect and the effect on the overall goal of the mission. The effect of a failed fuel pump, for example, is low fuel pressure. The effect on the mission is degraded operation or perhaps loss of propulsion, depending on other factors.
- Define the potential failure mechanisms. Why will they fail? What is the root cause of each failure? In the case of the fuel pump, the cause is old age.
- Define the likelihood for each failure mode. How likely is each mechanism to fail within the timeframe of the analysis? Choose the same timeframe for all likelihood decisions and, if desired, perform additional analyses for different timeframes. Just be sure each analysis has the same timeframe.
- Define a severity rating or consequence for each effect for each component failure mode. See the second column of Table 7.
- Calculate a risk factor for each failure mode. This is done for you if you use the accompanying spreadsheet. (http://TheReliableBoat.com/ExtraStuff)

Identify Potential Solutions
- Identify predictive monitoring techniques. How will you know you have a failure before you have an effect? Try to maximize the time before the full extent of the degradation.
- Identify a recommended action for each fault type. You can use redundancy, or carry a spare, tools, or something else that would lessen the probability or consequence of the failure mode.
- Determine which mechanism you want to address based on the calculated risks and your goals.

- Adjust the consequences and probabilities based on your solution. You can either wait until you implement the solution or simply keep track of solutions you want to implement.
- Continue to refine the analysis until you are confident you can achieve your goals. Adjust your risk values as needed until you feel comfortable with the results. Also, review the values with other trusted individuals to gain a more robust analysis.

Update the Risk Data
- Repeat the process periodically or whenever something changes on your boat. (at least yearly). A change in the state or configuration of the equipment should trigger an adjustment to the analysis. For example when a component is replaced with a new one the likelihood of failure is reduced (That is after the infant mortality period has past). This is an ongoing effort for the life of your boat.

- Analyze each piece of equipment or analyze a class of equipment and refine it for a specific instance. For example, you can perform the analysis for a general class of machinery like boats. Then an individual boat owner can refine the analysis for their individual specific boat. The boat owner can then perform the last step in the process that is to determine what they want to do about the identified risks of their specific boat. Any number of classes of equipment like cars, boats, buildings, chainsaws, etc can utilize the analysis.

FMRA Boat Example

The accompanying spreadsheet (http://TheReliableBoat.com/ExtraStuff) has a beginning of the analysis for a general class of "boat." Each line in the table identifies a potential problem resulting from a failure of a component with the associated subsystem and system. It is not the failure mode but rather the effect of the failure mode.

The fields in the accompanying spreadsheet have already been defined generally and each boat does not necessarily have each of the components. You might not have a Loran position finder, for example. Similarly each boat is not used for the same purpose. One boat, for example, might be used for sightseeing only on sunny afternoons while another is used to cross the Atlantic. Clearly the Captains of these boats will have different objectives. Enter the risk data as you refine the analysis for your particular boat and usage, for example: SYSTEM:

engine, SUBSYSTEM: cooling, COMPONENT: raw water pump, FAILURE MODE: cooling line clogged, Effect: degraded operation, etc. The definitions of each column is defined in Table 6 Review each entry, add and delete entries, and adjust risk values (likelihood and consequence). The spreadsheet will calculate the risk factor and risk levels for you. Use the spreadsheet sorting and filtering capabilities to sort and filter the results of your analysis. When finished, review the highest risk items and decide how you can mitigate the risk. The spreadsheet provides some suggestions but there are an infinite set of solutions, so you are encouraged to introduce some of your own

Table 6: Definition of the FMRA Data Fields

System	Identifies the system where the problem may occur
Subsystem	Identifies the subsystem where the problem may occur
Component	Identifies the component where the problem may occur
Failure mode	Defines what can actually go wrong with a component; for example, something can facture, leak, clog, degrade in performance, fail to operate, etc.
Failure mechanism – Cause	The failure mechanism defines why the failure mode can happen. You can get into great detail here and get down to the root causes of a failure. In some cases, the failure mechanism is operator error, and a root cause can be defined as follows: "The failure was caused by corrosion of the circuitry, caused by water leakage into the cabin, caused by a damaged seal, caused by old age and poor maintenance."
Effect	Here we define the effects. These effects should be tied to specific goals that are not met, such as loss of mobility, degraded operation, or irritant. If we keep the number of these to a minimum, we can report all the failure modes that will affect this goal.
Likelihood	The likelihood defines how likely it is for the effect to be realized. Now the likelihood is different for a 3-hour tour, a 7-day cruise, or the next 5 years. For the purpose of this example, we will use the next 5 years. The likelihood is a number from 0% to 100%, but can also be thought of as remote, unlikely, likely, highly likely, and near certainty as follows: 0 - 20% Remote 21 - 40% Unlikely

	41 - 60% Likely	
	61 - 80% Highly likely	
	81 - 100% Near certainty	
Consequence	Here we have to define 5 categories: .1 Loss of redundancy – a redundant component has been compromised so that the advantage of redundancy is lost .3 Degradation of operation – the capability or operation can still be performed but with some loss of speed or accuracy .5 Loss of capability – loss of some type of functionality but not mobility .7 Loss of mobility – Boat cannot be motivated in a desired direction .9 Fire, Flood, Loss of life – boat is sinking or on fire, or someone is in danger of serious injury or loss of life	
Risk Factor	The Risk Factor is a relative number calculated based on the likelihood and consequence numbers. The calculation skews the result so that the consequence is slightly more important than the likelihood. The calculation is 1-(1-consequence)^likelihood.	
Degraded operation	Yes or No: Will this effect potentially cause degraded operation?	
Dead in the water	Yes or No: Will this effect potentially cause loss of mobility?	
Directly dangerous	Yes or No: Will this effect potentially cause loss of life?	
Personally experienced	Yes or No: Have I personally experienced this problem?	
Redundancy – Stand-by	Yes or No: Can this problem be addressed with standby redundancy?	
Carry a spare	Yes or No: Can this problem be addressed by carrying a spare part?	
Monitor	Yes or No: Can we monitor to predict or diagnose the problem?	
Adjunct Device	Which devices or operations can we use to reduce the likelihood or the consequence of the problem?	
Notes	Any pertinent notes?	

Table 7: Captain's Objectives to Consequence Value Mapping

Objectives	Effects of Failure	Consequence Value
Prevent death	Death	.9 Fire, Flood, Loss of life
Prevent loss of property	Loss of ship	.9 Fire, Flood, Loss of life
Prevent sinking	Sinking	.9 Fire, Flood, Loss of life
Prevent fire	Fire hazard	.9 Fire. Flood, Loss of life
Maintain navigation lights	Loss of navigation lights	.7 Loss of mobility or safety
Maintain mobility	Loss of mobility	.7 Loss of mobility or safety
Maintain lubrication	Loss of mobility	.7 Loss of mobility or safety
Maintain fuel level	Loss of mobility	.7 Loss of mobility or safety
Keep vessel from grounding	Loss of mobility	.7 Loss of mobility or safety
Navigation redundancy	Loss of navigation redundancy	.5 Loss of capability or critical redundancy
Maintain critical redundancy	Loss of critical redundancy	.5 Loss of capability or critical redundancy
Maintain bilge system performance	Loss of dewatering capabilities	.5 Loss of capability or critical redundancy
Maintain electrical circuits	Loss of electrical circuits	.5 Loss of capability or critical redundancy
Maintain house battery	Loss of electrical circuits	.5 Loss of capability or critical redundancy
Maintain speed control	Loss of	.3 Degradation of operation

	speed control	
Maintain direction control	Loss of direction control	.3 Degradation of operation
Maintain full performance		.3 Degradation of operation
Maintain full-speed capability	Loss of full speed	.3 Degradation of operation
Maintain ease of starting	Hard starting	.3 Degradation of operation
Maintain engine performance	Poor performance	.3 Degradation of operation
Maintain cooling	Engine overheating	.3 Degradation of operation
Keep frustration level down	Irritant	.1 Loss of redundancy
Make passengers happy		.1 Loss of redundancy

Chapter 5: Steps to Increase Marine Reliability

A Systems Approach to Preventing Engine Failure

Without a working engine, everyone onboard is subject to the waves and the weather. Since a boat's engine is so important to the well being of the passengers and crew, it is surprising that they are so prone to failure. As a boat owner, take time to understand your engine systems and failure modes. Then take steps to decrease the chances an engine failure can occur.

Cooling-System Solutions

Without an operable cooling system, your engine will not get you back to port. Marine engine cooling systems are less reliable then automobile or truck cooling systems. This is mostly due to corrosion and the addition of a raw water pump, which pumps the surrounding water into the cooling system. If the intake gets clogged with debris, the pump itself is subject to failure.

Raw Water Flow

On a slightly chilly autumn afternoon, while my wife and I were sitting and reading in our docked boat, I noticed a commotion astern. Suddenly, there was a loud crash. A 40-foot Sea Ray had met the immovable pier head on. Fortunately, it was moving slowly. As I walked out of my boat to see if I could be of assistance, I noticed the large mass of the Sea Ray coming straight toward it, with a couple of teenagers trying to steer her straight. We barely managed to keep the boats apart. Was this person an idiot? Was this his first time maneuvering a boat at a dock?

I initially thought the boat had come away unscathed, but upon closer examination, the crash on the pier had driven the Sea Ray's stainless-steel anchor mount back into the bow. The operator of the vessel apologized profusely for getting so close to my boat, stating he had little control of the vessel because one of his engines had overheated and he was unable to maneuver the large craft. It is difficult to steer a twin-engine boat limping on one engine in a straight line, let alone maneuver it. This is a case where redundancy does not provide sufficiency.

The port engine of the 40-footer had overheated due to a broken raw water pump. It is fairly simple and inexpensive to replace the worn impeller because it is a standard maintenance item. So why did the pump break? Because unfortunately, many new boat owners do not know they have this standard maintenance item, let alone how to fix it. That was the case of this boat's new owner.

Flexible Impeller Pump

Most raw water pumps are flexible impeller vane pumps. The flexible impeller rotates inside a housing and flexes against a cam that drives the water under pressure through the raw water cooling system. Flexible impeller pumps are simple, self-priming, and work at a variety of speeds. They offer more flow per size and weight than other designs, and in good condition, they are ideal for boat engines. The one drawback is the impeller wears out or gets old and needs to be replaced. Old age will cause the impeller to lose its flexibility. When this happens, one or more of the vanes will stiffen or break off, resulting in a loss of pumping capacity. If the impeller is properly designed, it should be easily accessible for disassembly and inspection. This inspection needs to be done annually, and the impeller should be replaced every 2-5 years, whether it needs to be replaced or not.

Not all boats are designed for easy access to the raw water cooling pump. In some outboard and inboard/outboard engines, the flexible impeller pump is located below the water line, just above the lower unit. In these cases it is almost as expensive to check the pump as it is to replace it. If you are mechanically inclined, you can check it yourself;

otherwise you will have to pay a mechanic to replace it. The serious boater will replace a poorly located raw water pump with an external pump and place it in a location that is easy to access. This is usually on the front of the engine, and attached directly to the engine's crankshaft or driven with a v belt.

Some tips about flexible impeller pumps:

- Inspect or replace the impeller every 2 to 5 years.
- Replace the impeller when it gets worn or old. Stiffness or cracking often develops with age.
- Always carry an online spare raw water pump onboard.
- Add raw water flow sensors to determine if you are getting the proper flow.

Exhaust Manifold and Riser

They are usually made of cast iron and have hot water running through them. Cast iron corrodes. If you are running your boat in salt water, then you have hot salt water running through them. Cast iron corrodes rapidly in salt water. This is a maintenance item. Regular checking is in order here as is temperature and raw water flow monitoring.

When these cast-iron parts corrode, they clog up the internal passages used to transfer cooling water around the engine. When sufficiently clogged up, cooling water cannot get through to do its job; therefore, gradually heating the components until the engine overheats and you are stuck in the water with no propulsion.

There are several pieces of good news about the exhaust manifold and riser:

- This is usually a gradual problem that only affects your engine at the tail end of the degeneration.
- The cast iron parts can be cleaned out.
- The deterioration of the system can be monitored to ascertain the condition.

There is also some bad news, however:

- If the parts clog up badly, you cannot turn the engine.
- Marine exhaust cast iron parts are expensive.

- The engine temperature monitor that comes with your boat is the last indication of a clogged cooling water system. Engine temperature is either going to tell you that everything is ok, or to stop the boat now or you will cause damage.

As you will see in the next section, there are several ways to check the cooling system. You will want to monitor the raw water flow, exhaust manifold, and riser temperature. Every boat should have inexpensive temperature-indicator strips mounted on each manifold and riser. It is cheap assurance that the cooling system is working.

Early Warning for Cooling System Problems
Most people don't know:
- Marine cooling system degrade slowly
- The degradation can be measured and monitored

A weakened cooling system can be detected weeks or months prior to the actual overheating of the engine. This provides plenty of time to get it maintained while continuing to use the boat.

As an example, last summer one of my boats measured a higher than normal exhaust manifold surface temperature. Where I live, the summer is short and you need every advantage to use the summer while you have it. While I was concerned about it, I watched it but continued to use the boat all summer. Monitoring clearly showed the elevated temperature but the engine never overheated.

Since I had this advanced knowledge, I waited until a convenient time to have the system inspected and repaired. Turns out the raw water pump was wearing and didn't provide the optimum flow rate.

Most if not all boats come with an overheat sensor and monitor. When that monitor indicates overheating, you need to stop the engine. It probably won't be at the time and place that you choose.

Early warning sensors measure:
- Exhaust manifold surface temperature usually less than 140°F
- Exhaust riser surface temperature usually less than 140°F or 150°F
- Raw water flow rate. Depending on your boat.

Cooling System Monitoring

The sooner you detect a failure in the cooling system, the better. There are several places to monitor the cooling system. The difference in monitoring techniques is the speed at which you will get the information that something is wrong. Following is a list in order of "sooner" to "later":

- Raw water flow sensor
- Exhaust gas temperature
- Exhaust manifold and riser surface temperature
- Heat exchanger temperatures
- Cylinder head water temperature
- Steam or smoke coming from the engine compartment
- Engine stops running

At what stage would you like to know the condition of your system?

Raw Water Flow Sensor

While there are a few of methods of detecting water flow, only two are available for marine raw water cooling flow. Each will require installing a strainer prior to the sensor. This is important because a raw water strainer will filter out a certain amount of debris while still allowing water to flow. It usually has a clear housing so you can see when it needs cleaning. A raw water strainer is a good idea with or without a raw water sensor.

The two sensor types are: flow switch and flow rate sensor. The flow switch is less expensive and gives an indication of a certain flow rate. The problem with these is the rate of an idling engine is much less than a faster running engine. When a flexible impeller pump starts to fail, it will manifest itself at high speeds first. Unless the sensor is set for specific high flow rates, the flow switch will not detect the first signs of a weakening flexible impeller switch. It will, however, detect a full stoppage of the water flow that can happen if the system sucks up a large amount of debris. On the other hand, a flow rate sensor will detect a weakening of the system.

The flow rate sensor indicates the amount of cooling water flowing through the system in a certain amount of time, such as liters per minute or gallons per hour. This type of senor is an excellent choice for performance boats or for keeping track of a gradual weakening of the cooling water system.

A raw water flow sensor will provide the fastest indication of something stopping the cooling water flow.

Exhaust Gas Temperature

The exhaust gas in a marine engine is water cooled and, therefore, usually below 100° C. The best way to detect a problem is to install a temperature device into the exhaust gas flow. The best approach to all-temperature monitoring is to keep track of temperatures when the cooling system is in a known good state, such as when it has just been serviced. Then watch for temperatures exceeding those temperatures. This will tell you within seconds if cooling water is not being sufficiently supplied.

Exhaust Manifold and Riser Surface Temperature

Since the exhaust manifold of a marine engine is water-cooled, it should always be less than 60° C or 140° F, or 71° C or 160° F, depending on your engine. These sensors can be electronic, mechanical, or chemical. One inexpensive, accurate, and reliable method of surface temperature monitoring is the use of irreversible temperature indicators.

Irreversible temperature indicators will permanently change color one time if the temperature exceeds the defined amount. When operating an unknown boat, the first thing you should do is put several irreversible temperature tab values on the exhaust manifolds while operating and check to see that the temperature stays below 140°F.

Heat Exchanger Temperatures

Heat exchangers transfer the heat from the engine to the water outside the boat. This keeps the engine coolant clean and controls oxidation. The device has a raw water side and an engine coolant side. By monitoring the input and output temperatures of both raw water and coolant, you can calculate how much heat is being exchanged. The standard calculation is the Log Mean Temperature Difference, which is an indication of the magnitude of heat extraction.

You can install a heat meter that will indicate how much heat the heat exchanger is extracting. If the data is captured, it can be compared to optimal performance. Heat meters require 2 temperature probes and a flow sensor.

Cylinder Head Water Temperature Thermostat

This device helps keep your engine at the proper temperature. It closes while the engine is cooler than optimal running condition and opens when the engine is at proper operating temperature. Thermostats do fail. If you suspect a thermostat failure or you just want to eliminate the worry of it occurring, simply remove it and try running the engine without it. In most cases no damage will result from running the engine without a thermostat, on a short-term basis. Keep an eye on the temperature to be sure it does not overheat. Make sure you bring onboard an emergency thermostat housing gasket and tools for emergency repairs.

Ignition System Solutions

The ignition system provides a spark that explodes the fuel, thereby providing the engine power. The first thing to check when the engine won't start is the ignition. The first things to upgrade (if you have them) is the points and condenser to an electronic ignition system.

Points & Condenser

Points wear in two areas; the connection points become pitted and the bearing that rubs on the distributor cam wears down. If you have points you probably have an older engine, and you probably have a slight amount of rust on the distributor cam that exacerbates the wear of the bearing surface.

If your boat has ignition points:

- Inspect often. Never go on a long journey without checking them first.
- Always carry a spare set of points and the appropriate tools to replace them while at sea. Never go on a long journey without bringing a spare set.
- If possible, replace the points with an electronic ignition system. They are more reliable and inexpensive.

Other Ignition Component Considerations
The engine compartment of most boats is a hot humid place, the perfect environment for corrosion to develop. Always protect your ignition component connections with dielectric grease. This includes high voltage sparkplug wires, terminal connections, battery connections, and starter motor connections. You should also protect all electrical connections with dielectric grease—something that should always be in your onboard toolbox.

Ignition coils often fail in boats, so carry a spare coil with you, in case of emergency.

Some engines have an external ballast resistor, which often fails. Find out if you have one, determine where it is and which type it is, and keep a spare onboard. If you cannot see the ballast resister, it is located inside your ignition coil and included in your redundant ignition coil.

Fuel Solutions

Fuel can become contaminated, causing engine components to fail. Following are some ideas to keep your fuel and fuel system in working order.

Ethanol Fuel
Do not use ethanol in your fuel unless your boat and engine are specifically designed for it. Even then, I would try to stay away from ethanol in your fuel. It is not as stable as non-ethanol fuel and does not contain as much energy per volume. I can see no reason to use ethanol in the fuel of a marine engine.

Fuel Filter and Water Separator
Once while I was driving my boat with some large waves following astern, water entered my fuel tank via the fuel tank overflow. As we entered each swell, the significant splash up the bow caused water to drive into the fuel overflow. As the water was pumped into the fuel system, the engine failed. It was dark outside and there I was in large waves. I was, however, able to remove the water/fuel separator, empty out the water, and start my engine again. Fortunately, this occurred in fresh water. If it were in salt water, a tow might have been required.

Diesel engines and outboard motors can get a device that detects water in the fuel separator. With a water-in-the-fuel detector, I would have known ahead of time that I had a problem.

Remember the *Questar* disaster I introduced in the first chapter? Most likely, the owner could not start his engine because of water in the boat's fuel. Either he didn't have a water separator in the fuel system, or the one he had wasn't large enough. The owner would probably still be alive today if he could have kept his engine running using a simple water separator. Most boats come with a combination fuel filter and water separator. If yours does not, get one before you go out into the water again.

How to Prevent Diesel Fuel Contamination

When manufactured, diesel fuel is clean and uncontaminated. When it is transferred, shipped, and stored, however, it picks up contaminates, such as water, biological growth, foreign particulates, and wax formations. Such contaminates are more likely to be delivered to your fuel from a nearly empty storage tank. In this situation, the potential boundary layer between water and oil is stirred up, allowing more contaminates to enter your engine. These contaminates can cause your engine to fail prematurely, or cause temporary stoppage due to clogged fuel filters. Do not circumvent the degree of filtration in order to reduce the clogging, as the filters are there to protect the engine. In fact, if your secondary filter does not filter to 2 microns, you should probably buy a better filtration system.

Damage to the engine can vary depending on the formation of acid and varnishes in your engine. These formations can rob your engine of life and performance, or simply clog your filters prematurely; potentially leaving you stranded at an inconvenient location and time.

The number one contaminant in diesel fuel, or gasoline, is water. Normally, water can enter the fuel system by condensation found on the inside of the storage tank. This can occur in your own fuel tank, or any tank in which the fuel was stored or transferred. Additionally, water can enter through improperly configured tank vents and improperly maintained fuel caps. Whatever the means of incursion, you need to be able to remove the water from your fuel system.

Several commercial devices are on the market that will separate water from fuel. Some of them claim 99% water removal. Large truck fleets insist that water/fuel separators be a required component of new truck purchases. In a marine environment, these separators are even more important. If you find yourself with water in your fuel, take the proper precautions to remove it.

One way to get water out of fuel is to sink a disposable diaper into the fuel tank. The military has been known to use this little trick. Baby diapers have a substance that will suck up water, but no other substances.

There is another device for sucking the moisture out of the fuel. It is more convenient to use than a diaper but not as effective. If you send the device down the fuel fill opening, it will sit on the bottom of the tank. Make sure you attach a chain to the device so you can retrieve it later. The device can protect the tank for months, or even years, just as long as no water gets into it. When water gets into the fuel, a new contaminate starts to grow; this contaminate is biological growth.

Fungus, algae, and other microbial life live in water contamination and feed off the hydrocarbons in your fuel. If left unchecked, it can cause acid formation that will reduce component life and clog your fuel filters prematurely. If you suspect biological growth, the application of various biocides on the market will arrest the process. There are two basic types: water-soluble and diesel soluble.

Water-soluble biocides remain at the bottom of your tank and attack the growth in your water layer. If you have no water layer, they will just stay there, waiting for water and biologics to form, promptly destroying them before they cause a problem. Diesel soluble biocides become part of the fuel itself. So while diesel biocides are transferred with the fuel, water-soluble biocides stay with the tank.

Some diesel biocide products operate in both water and fuel. Whichever you choose, you should know which is which and what the benefits are.

Foreign particulates also come from multiple sources. They are usually easy to filter out with the standard diesel filters. This type of contamination does the greatest harm to component life. Be sure you have multiple stage filtrations consisting of a 30-micron primary filter and a 2-micron final filter. This will assure protection of downstream components.

Wax formation can be a problem in cold weather unless specially formulated fuel is used. This wax is the same type found in ordinary candles you probably have in your home. It forms microscopically and can prematurely clog fuel filters. As with biological growth, however, additives will keep this from happening.

Offline filtering or kidney loop filtration provides additional contamination removal. Many marinas offer offline filtration or "fuel polishing" by dragging a filter rack to your vessel and pumping the fuel through special filters to remove the contaminants and then put the fuel back into your tank. The process removes water and all the contamination types mentioned here. Seriously consider this type of service if you find any type of contamination in your tank.

Kidney loop filtration is an especially fine onboard filtration that continually sends fuel through a filter and back into the tank. Eventually all the fuel is cleaned prior to being used in the engine. Alternatively, operating a separate pump cleans the fuel whether the engine is running or not.

As you can imagine, diesel filters clog up and will render the engine useless without proper planning. Always bring extra filters with you. Based on your experience and usage, determine how many sets you need to bring, whether you bring 1 extra set, for example, or 50. When you leave port and enter into prolonged agitation of the fuel tanks, that's when you find out what's really in them.

Also, when you change your suction side (primary) filters, you are apt to introduce air into the fuel system. This often results in the engine stalling and hard restarting. If your batteries are strong and there is no danger of collision or grounding, this is not particularly a problem. If, however, you are in a situation where you really need propulsion in a hurry, you would best make provisions for that.

Commercial vessels have online, switchable filters with an auxiliary self-priming fuel pump just after the primary suction-side fuel pump. You can add a new filter on the offline side while the online side is filtering. The fuel pump can run for several seconds, sending its output back into the tank, thereby purging the line of air prior to switching in the alternate filter.

Fuel System Monitoring

See the section on filter monitors for additional details on specific monitoring devices.

Both gasoline and diesel fuel filters can use a fuel filter monitor on the suction-side filter to sense when the suction is too great, indicating a clogged filter. Similarly, monitoring fuel pressure can determine if the proper pressure is available. Low pressure can result from clogged lines, filters, or poor fuel pump performance.

Commercial "water in the fuel" detectors are available for diesel and outboard gasoline engines. They give an audible and/or visual indication that it is time to empty or replace your water/fuel separator. Water in fuel detectors provide valuable early warning that water is getting into the fuel stream.

This type of device will work for inboard gasoline engines as well, but they are considered unsafe.

Electric Fuel Pump

Fuel pumps fail, and having an online redundant means of pumping fuel is desirable. The easiest way to accomplish this is with an electric fuel pump.

While an auxiliary electric fuel pump can be useful for redundancy and to aid in starting when priming is required, there are some issues with using an electric fuel pump for gasoline in an enclosed environment such as a boat. All such issues have to do with leaks in an enclosed environment.

Since leaks in the pressure side of the fuel lines are worse when the engine is not running, install the electric fuel pumps so they will only operate when the engine is running or momentarily during starting. To accomplish this, use an oil pump switch and a momentary switch to power the electric fuel pump. If you are using the electric fuel pump as an auxiliary, you will need an additional bypass switch (see Figure 10 for a typical electric fuel pump wiring diagram).

Also, be sure to properly size the fuel pump for your particular engine. Fuel pressures that are greater than required for a particular engine, produce additional risk of leaks and subsequent fire. Figure 11 represents the amount of fuel required by the engine at Wide Open Throttle (WOT) for different HP ratings. Use the figure to size your electric fuel pump.

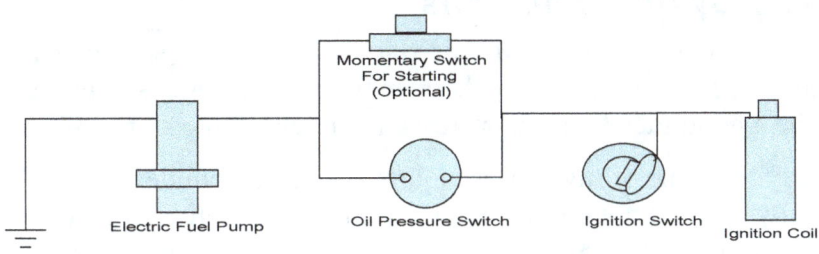

Figure 10: Electric Fuel Pump Wiring Diagram

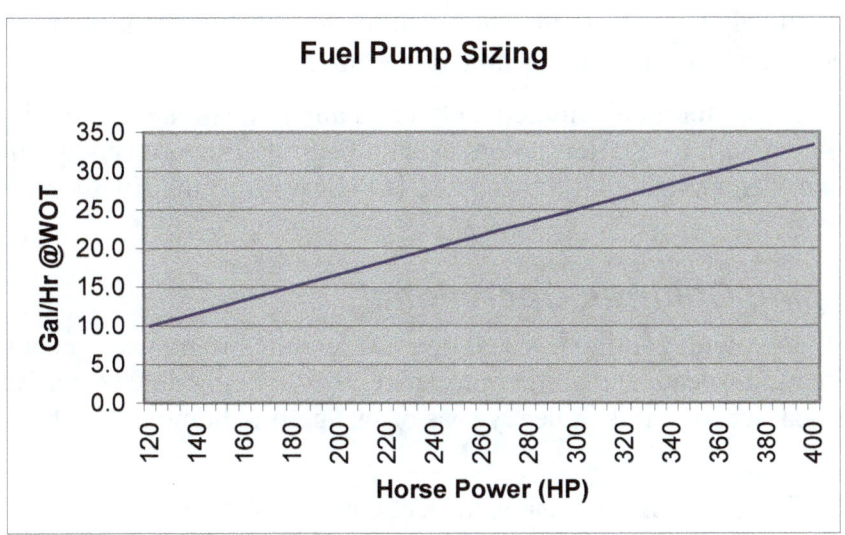

Figure 11: Fuel Pump Sizing

Spare Fuel Tank

It is always a good idea to have full redundancy. Even if you have redundant motors, if you also have contaminated fuel, they will do no good. It is always a good idea to have multiple fuel tanks and even a small auxiliary tank of fuel to get you safely ashore.

Starting System Solutions

While you can usually have Marine starters repaired, at sea you can only replace it with a new one if you happen to have a spare. Sometimes it might be a good idea to ask a professional to check the starter.

I recently took one of my starter motors into the re-builder to see if it was faulty. I could not get the engine to turn over well after it warmed up. As it turned out, the engine timing was too far advanced, causing slow cranking. The re-builder showed me the worn bearings in the starter, however, and suggested they be replaced. As a result, I am more confident that my starter is good and will not fail me for quite a while. I am thinking of replacing all the worn bearings for all my starter motors and alternators, in all my boats.

When putting a starter motor back together, always use dielectric grease. This will help keep the connections from corroding and heating up. Hot connections can cause fire or premature failure.

Replace a starter motor immediately upon any indication there might be a problem with it. Starter motors usually begin failing noticeably but still work enough to start the engine. Do not wait for the situation to get worse.

Keeping Controls Operational

It will do you no good to have an operable engine but no way to control it. Steering, speed, and shift controls are vital to being able to maneuver your boat whether it is in heavy seas or just getting home in a light breeze.

Depending on the mechanisms, inspect controls regularly. Have a plan in the event of failure. Some steering systems use cables that can be inspected. Others employ control wires inside another sheath. Still others use hydraulics to transfer helm commands to rudder or vector thrust. Whatever the mechanism, it can fail with the resultant issues, so plan for the possibility of losing one or more of your controls.

In most cases you could station someone below decks to manually fulfill the commands. Whether it be speed, steering, or shift, a vice grip and a walkie-talkie set would be useful here.

If an out drive or outboard engine is used, lines attached to the farthest aft points can provide emergency steering. A person holding the lines on each side port and starboard will provide the action. For the inboard boats, sometimes a bucket or sea anchor can be set astern and pulled from side to side to assist with steering.

Electronics Reliability

Voltage and power spikes are common on unprotected power busses and can damage critical electronic components. You should have a volt meter somewhere in your boat's electrical system. Normally, the voltage should never be greater than 20% over the voltage of the battery. In a 12V system, for example, the voltage should never be greater than 14.5 volts, which is about 12 volts + 20%. Over-voltage can occur if lightning strikes your boat. For more about lightning see the section on lightning protection.

Keep water and moisture out of electronics. If a particular device is not waterproof, as indicated in a manufacturer's claim, then protect it from direct access to waves and weather by placing them inside the cabin or under the dash. Moisture can attack electronics, however, even if the device never gets wet.

Corrosion on electronics occurs when water condenses on circuitry. After the condensed water collects a few ions from the environment, it becomes conductive and allows electromechanical reactions to start. This causes the metals on the circuit board to corrode or electricity to leak between conductors. So protect electronic circuits in a marine environment from moisture.

Place cell phones and other small electronics in zip lock bags and coat the electronics with a conformal coating. Conformal coating is a dielectric film that is "painted" on the circuit board. It hardens to a moisture- and abrasion-resistant coating. I have owned many electronic devices marketed as "Marine" that eventually corroded from too much moisture in the environment. So whenever possible I protect my electronics, except those designed to be water resistant like GPSs or sounders, with conformal coating. I especially recommend protecting radios and 12v to 110v inverters.

Electrical and Electronics

Electronics have become critical marine assets. We need them for communication, navigation, and monitoring. Keeping them in good condition requires some diligence. Corrosion is one of the primary reasons marine electronics fail. Following are some ideas on how to keep your electronics in good working order.

Dielectric Compounds

If you do not have dielectric compounds in your boating maintenance supplies, get some. They are the easiest and cheapest ways to add robustness to your electrical components. Two basic types of dielectrics exist: dielectric grease and dielectric liquid. The liquid sometimes comes in a spray can. Use the grease on large plugs, terminal blocks, and light bulbs, and use the lighter liquid for signal plugs such as those on your electronic plugs.

In the moist, harsh environment of the typical boat, whether in storage or on the open seas, water will condense on the metal of electrical and electronic components. This water becomes conductive and starts attacking metals through an electrochemical process. It is easy to control.

Here are some ways to control electrical corrosion:

- Lubricate every electrical connection, whether 110V, 12V, 3V, or less with a dielectric compound. Use grease on large connectors and liquid on small signal connectors.
- Coat every light bulb, battery, and fuse with dielectric grease. This includes flashlights.
- Coat the porcelain body of the spark plugs and on the exterior of the distributor cap posts. You can get special compounds for this at your automotive store, but I doubt they are much different from dielectric compounds. Use them if you like.
- If you can get inside switches, dab a little synthetic dielectric grease or liquid on the contacts to multiply its life expectancy.
- Do not forget your trailer wiring, connections, and light bulbs.
- Do not coat your GPS antenna connections. The grease might interfere with the high frequency signal, though there is some disagreement about this. Experts generally recognize a little dielectric liquid on the outside couple of threads will be OK, but no one really knows how the dielectric substance interferes at such high frequencies. It should be OK on VHF antennas, but always use it sparingly on any RF connection.

Dielectric compounds keep the moisture away from the metal and, therefore, eliminates corrosion. For light bulbs, spark plugs, and fuses, the dielectric compounds not only control corrosion but make it easier to change out.

Typically, when high-power connections, such as the voltage regulator or generator set terminals become corroded, their ability to conduct the necessary current through the connection degrades due to the higher resistance of the corroded connection. As this happens, the connection heats up and degrades it further. This causes more heat, which eventually ruins the device and perhaps causes a fire.

In lower-power applications, the corrosion again degrades the connections and eventually interferes with the proper working of the device. Eventually you have another failure. If it has happened to me, it can happen to you. It is simple to fix, however.

Clean and coat every electrical connection you can with the proper dielectric compound. Take the connection apart, clean it if it is already corroded, put a little dielectric compound on it, and re-apply the connection. The dielectric compound will not interfere with the connection and will not cause stray currents to adjacent connections or grounds.

I have seen entire sections of computer circuit boards coated with dielectric grease. This might be more expensive and not as good as conformal coating, but it is fast and easy.

This simple solution will provide the biggest bang for your maintenance time and buck.

Conformal Coating

As previously discussed, electronic components are susceptible to corrosion due to high humidity marine environments. If water condenses on the circuit boards, it does not take much to add the necessary ions to make them conduct electricity. When this happens, your electronics will not work properly. You might also damage components and start the corrosion process that will eventually cause your electronic device to completely fail. Conformal coating is a simple, complete cure for this type of degradation. Conformal coating might even take a direct hit from rain or waves and still protect the circuits.

Applying conformal coating is simple if you are handy enough to get an electronic circuit out of the case and back in again. It is a simple matter of cleaning the circuit board, then painting the board with a dielectric conformal coating. You can spray it, brush it on, or dip it. Brushing is the simplest and best approach for one-at-a-time circuit board coating.

Several types of conformal coating exist. Acrylic, epoxies, silicones, and urethane based are the most popular types. When you select a product, consider ease of application, ease of repair, and availability. Most conformal coatings have a UV dye that "lights up" under a black light for inspection purposes.

- Acrylic coatings provide an easy application (one part and no heat required), fast drying, and excellent moisture protection. They are also easy to remove and allow easy repair of the circuit board if repair is required.
- Epoxies are not good under extreme temperatures but exhibit good chemical and abrasive resistance. Epoxies are impossible to remove without damaging the electronics. Forget repairing.
- Urethane provides excellent abrasive and chemical protection, but is hard to remove if repair is required.

- Silicone coatings are good with thermal extremes and good at protecting components from vibrations but are difficult to remove if repair is needed and cure better with some heat. They are also more expensive than the other choices.

Any of the conformal coatings will work fine for the marine environment but the acrylic coatings provide the best balance between protection, cost, and ease of repair. Since you will probably not need to protect your components against chemical attack or abrasion, you might as well use the easy and inexpensive acrylic coating.

How to Put Conformal Coating on your Marine Electronics

The procedure consists of the following:
- Disassembly
- Cleaning
- Coating
- Reassembly

Disassembly

Take the device apart to the point that you can access the circuit board that needs protection. Remove it if possible but if you can't do the best you can.

Cleaning

In order for the coating to adhere to the surface of all components, the surfaces must be free from grease, flux, dirt, dust etc. Cleansing is accomplished by scrubbing with an appropriate solvent. Use a small paintbrush, making sure to get underneath all components. Denatured alcohol is a good solvent for cleaning prior to coating.

Allow the board to completely dry before coating.

Coating

- Do **NOT** coat heat sinks, connectors, or any other components that will be affected by the coating.

- Do **NOT** coat anything that needs to move freely or that needs optical access, like a light sensor, or that needs to fit precisely into something.
- Do **NOT** use conformal coating on connectors; instead coat them with a dielectric compound as discussed previously.
- If you are in doubt, do **NOT** coat it. Use common sense when determining what to coat.

Apply the coating with a small brush just like the one you used when you cleaned your circuit board. This will help you avoid getting coating on the parts that should not be coated.

Beginning at one end, coat the entire side of the circuit board. Then turn your component over and coat the opposite side.

Some conformal coating material glows under ultraviolet light. This allows you to check your work by viewing the circuit board under a black light. Areas that were not coated will not "light up."

Allow the board to dry completely before reassembling it.

Reassembly

After its dry, put everything back together and you're done.

Congratulations! You have just increased the reliably of your electronic device.

Charging System

- Use a built-in generator set or a portable generator.
- Multiple engines should take advantage of multiple battery-charging systems.
- Solar and wind
- Shore power charging

Similar to the starter motor, if the alternator fails while at sea, you must replace it. Having a spare will greatly increase your chance of getting back home. You might be able to get a re-builder to fix it. Usually, the bearings fail. A re-builder can easily replace them.

Alternator failure affects two areas. The first area is the ability to produce 12V electricity. Having an auxiliary gen-set allows you to generate electricity without your primary alternator.

The second thing alternator failure affects is the ability to cool the engine. On most marine engines, the alternator is turned with a rubber V belt or serpentine belt. This belt often turns other components like power steering and the cooling recirculation pump. Each of these components relies on the others to hold the drive belt so each of them can obtain power. If the alternator bearings fail, for example, the belt cannot spin and, therefore, the cooling pump cannot operate. Often you can use an emergency belt that will adjust to leave out the failed component, thereby allowing the other components to turn. Inspect the configuration of your drive belt and determine if you can use one of these emergency adjustable belts.

As with all electrical connections on the boat, protect alternator connections from corrosion with dielectric grease.

Battery recharging is a critical function of the systems in any boat. Redundancy is the key issue for charging.

If you have 2 engines and 2 alternators, be sure you have the ability to cross between them to start the alternate engine in case of a failure. A high current relay usually provides this capability.

Additionally, an onboard generator set will provide the needed redundancy. If your engine-charging system fails, you can switch over to your generator set.

There are many different configurations for batteries and charging. Do you have one engine with an additional generator set? Do you have solar or wind charging? You might have multiple engines with multiple alternators with multiple batteries on each charging circuit. Whatever the case, understand what your situation is and keep up on it.

Battery

Key points for better battery reliability
- Redundancy
- Keeping batteries charged
- Keeping terminals clean and using dielectric grease
- Replacing the battery at the right time

You are dead in the water without a simple charged battery. It stores electricity so you can start your engine and operate your emergency and other electronic equipment. It should not be taken lightly; maintain a healthy battery and a healthy charge on the battery. Know the state of your battery with the necessary volt and amp meters. This is a case where redundancy, monitoring, and control are the key issues.

When I used the word "simple" in conjunction with the battery, I was not referring to the complexity of the choice of batteries. Depending on what you expect from the battery, you will need a different type of battery. There are starting batteries and there are deep cycling batteries. As you might expect, the starting battery starts your engines. These batteries should be separate from auxiliary batteries that, for example, operate your bilge system when the engine is not running. The deep cycle batteries operate your low-voltage system devices when the engine is off.

If discharged too often, damage to starting batteries results. In fact, degradation of deep cycle batteries also occurs when discharged too much. All lead acid batteries should be kept to as close to 12V as possible to get the maximum life out of them.

Deep cycle batteries are large and expensive. I am not talking about the marine deep cycle batteries you can buy in the car parts store that say "Marine Deep Cycle." These batteries are OK for light-duty jobs, but if you are going to use the 12V system for extended duty, get some of the large and expensive deep cycle batteries.

Consider redundancy for the engine starting battery. In order to keep from being stranded, the battery for "house" usage should not be the battery used to start the boat. If the house battery runs out of charge, you can charge it up as long as you can start the engine. If you cannot start the engine, however, you need an additional emergency procedure like an emergency battery pack.

The issue with having two battery buses is that each discharges separately but both charge with the same alternator or gen. set. There needs to be a means of separation. You can use a special 2-battery switch or a battery buss isolator. The buss isolator is automatic and does not require the operator to do anything. On the other hand, a battery switch requires the operator to switch the alternate buss off when the engine is not running. There are several devices on the market for just such a function.

In some cases, you might want to use the "house" battery as additional power for engine starting. If you use a simple battery buss switch, you automatically have the power from both batteries when the buses are switched together. If you are using an isolator, you will need a manual switch to bring the two buses together for emergency starting. In most cases, you will want a high-current relay triggered by a momentary on switch. The relay allows the switching of high-current wires with a low-current switch. The momentary trigger switch requires the operator to hold the switch on during operation to assure the switch will not be left on by mistake.

Emergency Battery Pack

An emergency battery pack is always a good thing to have in case your starting battery fails. Another use for an emergency battery pack is to bypass the starter relay in the event that it fails. Just put the black wire to ground then place the red wire directly to the starter. Keep in mind that this is potentially hazardous as it will cause a spark which could ignite gasoline fumes in the bilge if they are present. Also be careful not to touch any other ground with the red lead.

Chapter 6: Preventing an Emergency

Fire

In November 2000, a routine voyage of *The Port Imperial Manhattan* [27], a small passenger vessel, left passengers stranded and the boat extensively damaged. Three crew members and eight passengers were aboard that evening when a fire broke out in the engine room, despite the fact that hourly watches were set and kept to inspect the engine room. While eating dinner, the Master noticed smoke coming from a vent to the engine room. A deck hand assessed the situation while the Master radioed for help to stand by. Shortly after the Master sent the message, the engine, steering, and power to the radio failed.

Crew members tried to extinguish the blaze with handheld firefighting apparatuses, but with no success. The crew received electrical shocks while opening the engine room door, which inhibited firefighting. After a short time, the smoke was so thick the crew could not enter the room.

As the thick smoke forced passengers outside the passenger compartments, they were instructed to stay in the boat, but never asked to put on PFDs. Help arrived, rescued the passengers, and towed the badly burning boat to shore. Local firefighting teams eventually extinguished the fire, while the passengers narrowly escaped as flames engulfed the *Port Imperial Manhattan* approximately 30 seconds after the passengers were aboard the rescue boat.

A loose electrical connection inside a terminal box caused the fire, and an open-access door allowed it to spread to other areas of the boat. The boat had no automatic fire-detection system or a fixed fire-suppression system installed.

What can we learn from the *Port Imperial Manhattan* fire?

Proper electrical installation and maintenance are critical to reliable boating.

A fire-detection system in the engine room would have alerted the crew much earlier and might have allowed handheld fire suppression to be effective.

A fixed fire-suppression system would have been more effective in fighting the fire since the crew could not even get near it due to heavy smoke.

Passengers should have been instructed to don PFDs because this was an emergency.

Fire assessment should be a critical part of emergency procedures. Had the rescue vessel been 30 seconds later, passengers would have been either burned or been forced into the water without proper personal floatation equipment. In most cases it is better to stay with the boat, but in some cases it would be better to abandon ship, or at least be ready to.

Fire Response

Marine Accident Report, Fire on Board the Small Passenger Vessel *Seastreak New York* Sandy Hook, New Jersey September 28, 2001, NTSB/MAR-02/04 PB2002-916404

> The *Seastreak New York* responded beautifully to a potential disaster on September 28, 2001. The fire damaged the vessel but did not destroy it due to proper firefighting equipment and procedures.
>
> A fire broke out in the main engine room, causing the mate that discovered the fire to flee from the room for lack of breathable air. The crew manually secured all vents and hatches and initiated the onboard CO_2 fire-suppression system from the control room.
>
> The fire caused the starboard engine to fail but the *Seastreak New York* was able to get to shore using its port engine. All passengers disembarked and a fire crew assessed the fire. The CO_2 fire suppression system extinguished the fire. There were no reported injuries but extensive damage to the starboard engine resulted.

The cause of the fire was simple and easily avoidable—improper installation of an auxiliary lube oil system. A flexible hose was installed too close to a hot exhaust manifold, resulting in a rupture and oil spill. This should have been caught during installation, or subsequently as a part of routine maintenance inspection. Always think in terms of what "could" happen.

Several important points are evident from this incident:

- The engine room was periodically monitored, which was instrumental in discovering the fire in time to take action before it spread.
- The permanent installation of the CO_2 fire suppression system and proper training was critical to controlling the fire. Install all equipment properly according to the manufacturer's instructions, as well as common sense.
- Periodic maintenance inspection should reach beyond the norm. Inspectors should think about everything that could possibly happen: *Are any installations showing signs of change? What would happen if...?*

According to internet statistics, the majority of fires that occur aboard boats come from short circuits. This is good news because this is an area we can almost completely eliminate with good design and maintenance.

The next most common cause of boating fires is engines overheating. Again, with proper monitoring and maintenance, you can nearly eliminate the incidence of overheating.

Instead of going into further detail about what can happen in a fire, I suggest you visit the *Boat US Seaworthy* web site noted above. Their parent company is a marine insurance company that has investigated many marine fires. The results are there for your benefit.

Electrical Fires

The following is a posting on the Chris Craft Commander web site from the owner of a 41-foot Chris Craft Commander named "Shindig":

> "Group,
>
> Just a heads-up on a potentially dangerous situation that just happened on Shindig night before last.
>
> I was running on the genny *(generator)* for a while after having installed a new belt and spark plugs. After 30 minutes I started smelling a burnt plastic scent. It took me 20 minutes of sniffing and looking everywhere from the engine room to the

cabins/staterooms. I finally found the smell coming from the disconnect/breaker box to the genny feed. In fact the 70 amp breaker and box labeled 'Breaker Light Plant' was almost too hot to touch!!!
After shutting all electrical down, I unscrewed the faceplate and found the
feed neutral roasted and toasted about the last 4 inches. The insulation was almost completely burned off! After investigating the damage and determining the cause................(guess the $$$ spent at State Fire school and 15 yrs. as a Volunteer Firefighter finally paid off???)

I determined the wires feeding the breaker were loose and not able to pass the required 60-70 amps when the genny is loaded to the max. There is no telling how long this had been happening and progressively getting worse every time the genny was run.

After fixing the problem, I checked all the connections in every breaker box and found almost every screw/clamp took a minimum of 1 full turn to tighten completely!

Bottom line is..................... check and tighten all your 120-volt
connections in your boat. With the combination of age, vibration, and moisture there may be loose connections in your breaker boxes that can heat up when you approach the load limit of your shore power and/or genny output.

Luckily I caught this just in time and only had to replace the disconnect/breaker. This could have been a mess had I not smelled the burning wires!!!

By the way, before checking your breaker connections .... Be safe and shut down and unplug your shore power cords; then use a medium to large screwdriver to get the torque needed to tighten down the large feed wiring clamps.

Shindig
1973 Commander 41 Flush Deck w/427 power

Mark Hunter"

Water and moisture is the electrical system's worst enemy. Moisture causes corrosion that can raise the resistance on the electrical connection that makes heat, which can cause a fire.

In this case the electrical terminals could have been protected by dielectric grease and checked for tightness.

Fire Detectors

A couple of years ago while I was working on a ship automation system for the U.S. Navy, they gave us a tour of their newest aircraft carrier. The ship was so new that the bleachers they used for the dedication were still up. The ship was huge. I asked the Captain, "How many smoke or fire detectors do you have onboard?"

He replied, "Today we have 2,732 smoke detectors onboard," referring to the number of crew members aboard that day. The U.S. Navy does not use smoke detectors because apparently they do not trust them. Instead, they have many people aboard who are trained in at least rudimentary emergency fire procedures. You do not have this luxury. Get fire detection and suppression onboard your vessel.

Wiring

All wiring in a boat should be neat in order to facilitate easy diagnosis of problems as well as system upgrades. Additionally, the more crossed, loose wires you have the greater potential you have of causing a short circuit. As we discussed in a previous section, short circuits are the major cause of boat fires.

Flood – Dewatering (Bilge Pump System) Reliability

The *Panther* was a small sightseeing boat used in the Florida Everglades. It was poorly operated and poorly maintained. The boat had a shaft tunnel that protected the propeller and allowed the boat to navigate shallow waters. Even though it was common for these types of boats to run aground, it should not be OK to run aground without inspection and maintenance afterward as the operators of the Panther did.

The *Panther* was running in a damaged state for an extended period without repair. The boat was taking on water regularly. The bilge pumps masked the symptoms, and the problem got worse until the final day. Adding to the potential problem was a corroded and inoperable bilge high-water alarm. Additionally, the starboard bilge pump did not work.

The *Panther* was on its third tour of the day. The operator, who indicated the boat had been operating fine, noticed no problems. One of the passengers, while waiting to board, noticed the port bilge pump was pumping out water on a regular basis. He estimated 3 or 4 gallons every 30 seconds, though he said nothing until after the voyage.

About halfway through its last tour, the *Panther* listed to the starboard side. So much water spilled over the sides that the Master stopped the boat and flagged down a passing crab boat for assistance. As soon as the crab boat pulled alongside, the *Panther* swamped and sank right out from under the passengers.

The *Panther* had been operating in a damaged state. The section of the hull that held the propeller strut was broken, rotted, and leaking water. As it got worse, the leaking increased. Only one of the two bilge pumps was working and the high water alarm was not operable.

Even though no deaths resulted, the accident should have been avoided.

- The boat should have been thoroughly inspected after the initial grounding. That would have uncovered a weakness in the attachment of the propeller strut.
- The high water alarm should have been tested and fixed.
- The starboard bilge pump should have been tested and fixed.
- The passenger who noticed the bilge pump running excessively should have mentioned it to the Master. Better still, a bilge pump counter or flow integrator would have given the master the required information.
- The boat should never have been allowed to operate using the bilge pumps to mask a serious hull leak.

Similar things can happen to you, for example:

- Your out-drive bellows leaks, causing a small, but continual, leak. Un-noticed, you leave the boat at the dock for an extended period. The periodic bilge pump cycles wears down the battery until it is dead. The next time you return to the boat, it is below water.
- Your engine backfires, blowing a hole or knocking off the exhaust hose, causing cooling water to fill your bilge. You don't notice it, however, and continue on your voyage until you notice the boat acting sluggish. Your ability to overcome this incident without sinking depends on the configuration of your boat and bilge pump capacity.

- A through hull fitting becomes loose and allows a continual accelerating leak into your bilge. You might sink while you are underway or at the dock, or you might discover the leak in time to fix it before the sinking occurs.

- Your stern docking line falls overboard and wraps around your propeller, bending the shaft that continues to rotate long enough to smash a good-sized hole in your hull. Without significant emergency bilge pumps, you will surely sink.

- You get caught in a large rainstorm with high winds and waves, which cause you to take waves over the bow, stern, or gunwales. Bilge pump capacity is critical here to get the water out of the boat before more water comes in. Remember sinking accelerates as your boat gets lower in the water. Large waves over the bow can break out the windshield and make the situation worse.

- Loss of a propeller shaft or rudder leaves a large hole in your boat. Emergency bilge pump capacity and a way to temporarily plug the hole is what is needed here. Without them, you will sink rapidly.

Table 8: Why Boats Sink

Reason Boats Sink While Underway	
Taking Water Over the Gunwales:	30%
Leaks at Thru-hulls:	18%
Leaks at Raw water Cooling System/Exhaust:	12%
Drain Plug Missing:	12%
Navigation Error (Grounding):	10%
Boat Construction (Hull Split Open):	6%
Leaks at Out-drive Boots:	4%
Struck Floating Debris:	4%
Other:	4%

Table 8 shows why boats sink. These situations happen often. If you have people onboard who are weak swimmers, a situation can become even more dangerous. Adequate pumping capability is crucial. How much is enough and how much is too much? The answer is simple: you cannot have too much emergency pumping. Determining the minimum requirement is more difficult. First you must determine the kind of boat you have and the way it is used. If you have an open bow and take it offshore 25 miles or more, you will need more than the person who has a closed bow and only travels around inland lakes when the weather is nice. Even the inland boat must be prepared for an unexpected storm. Many boats have multiple compartments. Each of these is treated separately with its own bilge pump system.

The bilge pump system is your lifeline, and in many cases it's more important than a life raft. Don't take it lightly. Let's talk about what can and does happen that might require you to get a good bilge pump system. Even though most sinking occurs at the dock, the bilge pump system should be designed for the worst-case scenario at sea, not the best-case scenario at the dock.

Leaks can occur from several different components onboard. According to the *Boat US Seaworthy* web site[17], boats sink because of water over the gunwales; leaky through hull fittings; leaks from the raw water cooling system; leaks in out drive boots; rain, snow and sleet.

Repair or replace leaky through hull fittings immediately. In some cases the through hull is not being used and could be removed. Obviously, fill the hole with something. Either repair it with fiberglass or a dummy fitting.

According to ABYC, every below water through hull water fitting must employ a valve to shut off the flow of water in for emergency and maintenance. This is called a seacock. Just because you have one, does not mean it is in working condition. You must actuate it often to make sure it is working and not leaking. Take each seacock apart, inspect it, and lubricate it as part of your yearly maintenance. Replace any worn seals and parts, lubricate with water-resistant grease, and generally make sure the valve is in good operating order.

- Inspect through hull fittings regularly and repair or replace if necessary
- Inspect the condition of the hull around underwater through hull fittings. These can become loose or rotten and should be repaired immediately.
- Inspect, lubricate, and repair all sea cocks during yearly maintenance activities.

The raw water-cooling system is another major area that can cause excess water in the bilge. Raw water coming from a faulty exhaust system can fill the bilge and sink the boat before you know it. In many cases, the exhaust boot comes off or splits, causing large amounts of cooling water to enter the bilge. This happens many times as a result of engine backfiring. Inspect all the flexible components of your raw water-cooling system. Keep the engine in good running condition so you won't get any backfiring. Use double stainless steel clamps on all raw water fittings, including the flexible exhaust hoses.

One of the most important things to know is the rate your boat is taking on water, and whether the rate is increasing. Most boats leak some amount of water. You need to know what is normal and what is abnormal. Whether you know what the actual rate is, or whether you know how often the bilge pumps turn on, you should have some type of monitoring system.

The sinking of a boat will accelerate as it goes down. The lower the boat gets, the more above-water fittings and scuppers are underwater with the potential greater intake of water.

Consider a 2-inch hole in the bottom of your boat as a design goal. Figure 12 shows how much water will come in through a 2-inch hole at various depths. Two inches is about the size of a through hull Sonar transducer. If your hull bottom is 1 foot below the surface, for example, you can expect to fill a 55-gallon drum with water every minute from the 2-inch hole in the hull. That translates to 55*60 = 3300 GPH.

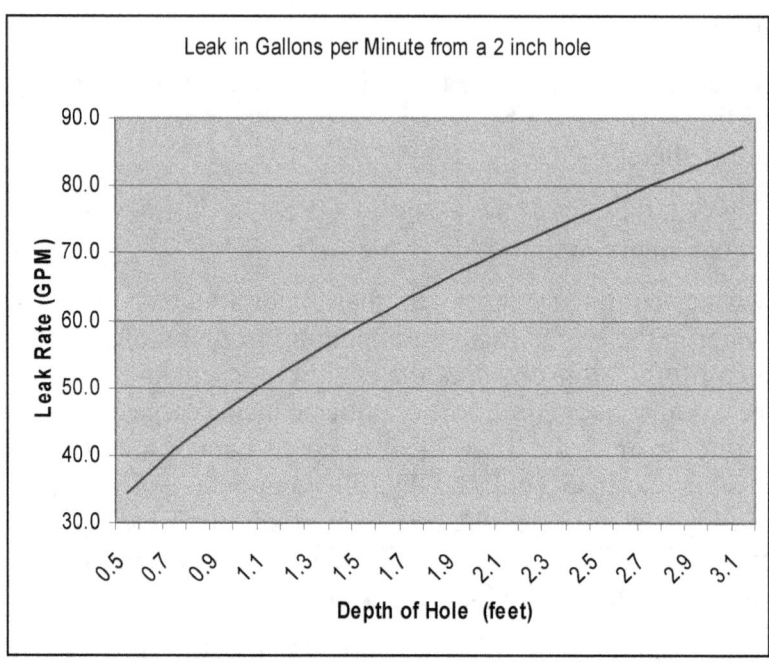

Figure 12: Leak Rate from a Two-Inch Hole

Add this all up and you have a disaster coming at you. The faster you respond, the less impact it will have.

You need ample bilge pump capacity, advanced indication of an emergency, and properly installed and inspected through hull fittings. Fifty-five gallons per minute is the same as 3300 gallons per hour; therefore, 4000 gallons per hour should be the least bilge pump capacity you should have in a boat that can expect a 2-inch hole a foot below the surface. Twice this rate should be a design goal of a good redundant system. In other words, this situation should have two independent 4000GPH bilge systems.

I know of a boat owner who took out his through hull SONAR transducer for inspection and decided to leave it out until a later date. Of course he forgot about the lack of a transducer the next time he launched the boat. It was a large trailer boat so he didn't realize it was taking on water at a rate of 55 gallons per minute until a couple of minutes had passed. This owner (name withheld) had already parked the car and disengaged the large trailer when he returned to the boat to see water on the deck. Rushing back to get the trailer hooked up, he neglected to latch it properly. He barely got the boat on the trailer, so it was cantilevered on the end. He pulled the boat out, and as soon as he stopped, the trailer popped off the hitch; swung on the safety chains; and ran smack into the back of the SUV, smashing in the back door. The boat was now resting, full of water, on the 2 bronze propellers. I understand it took 6–10 big men to get the trailer back on the hitch since the boat was hanging off the end.

This person was lucky. No permanent damage to the boat, but his pride needs a little more time to fully recover.

One of the most-often occurrences of bilge flooding for trailered boats is forgetting to put the drain plug in. I have done it more that once; almost everyone who trailers their boat at some time forgets this silly little plug. Certainly as a bare minimum, have enough pumping capacity to fully handle the loss of the drain plug. See Figure 13 for the rate of a 1-inch-diameter leak. As you can imagine, the 1-inch hole is quite a bit less than the 2-inch hole. If you meet the 2-inch-hole criteria, you will have this covered.

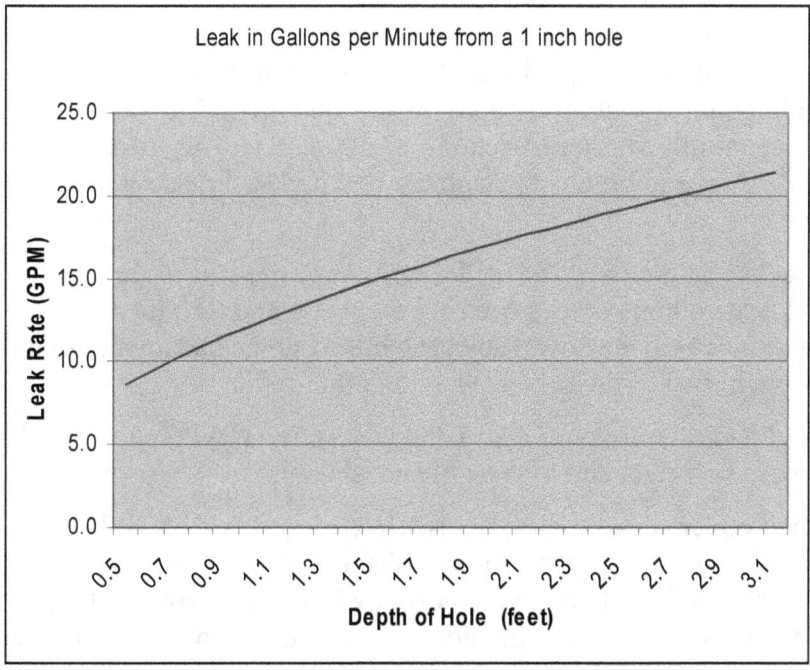

Figure 13: Rate of Leak vs. Head (Depth) from a One-Inch Hole

Leak Rate Calculation [30]:

$Q = 25*A*K*sqrt(h)$

Where:

Q is the leak rate in Gallons Per Minute (GPM).

A is the area of the hole in the boat.

K is a constant based on the configuration of the orifice I used .62.

h is the head of water. This head is the difference between the water in the boat and the water outside the boat.

sqrt(x) is the square root function for the quantity x.

Bilge Pump System Failure

The *Miss Majestic*[25] was a small military vessel converted for commercial sightseeing. It was built for rough duty and could remain afloat even if battle damage caused considerable leaking. This robustness was mostly due to an oversized bilge pump that received its power from the main engine.

The converted bilge system consisted of 3 small electric bilge pumps with a total pumping capacity of 2,500 GPH and the oversized engine-driven bilge pump with a capacity of 15,000 GPH. The total bilge system capability was a respectable 17,500 GPH. This vessel could have taken several bullets through the hull and still made it to shore safely.

The practice of the operator on the *Miss Majestic* was to turn on the electric bilge pumps before entering the water and turn them off when exiting. Since only one of the electric bilge pumps had an automatic float switch, two of the pumps were on all the time.

The boat had a shaft cover below the waterline. It was made of rubber and secured on each end by a single hose clamp.

The shaft cover somehow came off while in route with a full complement of passengers aboard. Water gushed in through a significant-sized void. No one knew anything was wrong until the boat listed to one side. Almost immediately the stern went under and the boat went to the bottom, stern first. The boat sank so fast that not all the passengers could get their life jackets on, and the operator could not even get out a May-Day message.

This was a failure to properly configure, monitor, and maintain. Proper configuration would have provided double clamps for the shaft cover as well as a proper bilge system. Monitor the amount of water in the bilge, the amount of water being pumped out, and the condition of the bilge system. Maintain the bilge systems as well as the vessel itself.

As it turns out:

- The boat had a small, continual leak that was ignored. It was small enough to be handled by the electric bilge pumps, but became large during its last voyage. Two pumps were on all the time, which totally masked the size of the leak.
- Two failed pumps significantly degraded the bilge system performance. One of the electric bilge pumps was broken, while the oversized bilge pump was not even connected. The resulting system capacity was 1750 GPM, just 10% of its full capacity.
- The vessel did not have the required high bilge water alarm sensor and alert indicator.

This catastrophe could have been avoided if:

- The operator was able to monitor the amount of water being pumped out of the bilge. The rapidly increasing rate would have provided advanced indication that the boat was taking on water.
- The bilge system was in proper working order.
- The cover that came off was properly maintained and tightly secured with redundant clamps.

More time could have been provided to allow the vessel to get ashore and better prepare passengers for the emergency:

- If the large bilge pump had been operable, it would have provided significant and critical time afloat.
- If the vessel had been equipped with a high bilge water alarm, it would have alerted the operator of the emergency and perhaps provided precious minutes of preparation time.
- If the third electric bilge pump had been operable, it might have allowed the boat to stay afloat a short time longer. Instead of 1,750 GPH, it would

have had 2,500 GPH of working bilge pump capacity and maybe stayed afloat long enough for the passengers to get on their PFDs.

This was a tragic account that could have been prevented with proper configuration, monitoring, and maintenance.

Whenever you have a continual, significant leak, get it fixed. Do not rely on the bilge system. Most boats have small leaks that are considered normal. As a rule of thumb, a small normal leak should be less $1/10,000^{th}$ the capacity of a redundant bilge pump system. Assume, for example, you have two redundant 1000 GPH bilge pumps. That gives you 2000GPH but only 1000 redundant GPH. 1/10,000 of that would be .1GPH or 2.4 gallons per day. Even if you left your boat unattended for 2 weeks, you would only have 33 gallons of extra water in the bilge. Most likely it will not be a problem as long as you maintain your battery, you don't get huge rainfall, and the leak stays small.

Monitoring the leak will give you an indication of how large the continual leak is and whether it is increasing. There are several devices on the market that tell you how many times the pump has turned on. Some actually give you the amount of time the pump was on.

Keep your bilge pumps in constant working order, and test them regularly. I'm sure the operator of *Miss Majestic* had no idea the bilge system was going to be called on for special duty on the day of that last voyage.

Bilge pumps are usually inexpensive plastic pumps that work pretty well most of the time; however, they have many failure modes with many causes. The motor jams due to contamination in the bilge, the hoses can become clogged due to junk in the bilge, the bilge float switch can become stuck due to floating debris, or the hose can crack or leak at the joint, just to name a few. The chances of your bilge pump system failing is great; therefore, you need redundancy and enough pumping capacity to overcome a large leak.

Many boats have minimal bilge dewatering capacity. The capacity should be a function of the size of the boat as well as the size of your through hull fittings. If you have four, 2-inch through hull fittings, you should have more pumping capacity than a boat that has a single 1-inch through hull fitting.

Inspecting and testing the bilge system is also important. A friend of mine took out a bareboat charter for the weekend. It was a fairly new 35-foot sailboat. As long as the boat was keeled over on the starboard side, it had no problems. But after a couple of hours into the sailing, the boat came about and keeled over on the port side. After a little while, those onboard noticed water on the floor of the cabin.

The boat had two bilge pumps, one on the port side and one on the starboard side. The port side exited the starboard aft and the starboard side exited the port aft. The hoses were armored with stainless steel braid, but each one ran through a stowage compartment. Apparently, the hose on the port side had broken right at the through hull fitting. When keeled over to the port, water gushed in faster than the port bilge pump could pump it out. Once the Captain determined the problem, he realized he could only sail keeled over to the starboard. This would not allow the boat to get back home until the problem was fixed.

While underway, the crew made the repair, good as new. The person who designed such a situation, however, should be flogged. This is just one example of what can happen. Had those onboard not been on their toes, the situation might have been worse.

They could have used an emergency bilge pump if they'd had one. These systems are usually powered by gasoline and provide an extra amount of bilge pumping in case of an emergency. One type uses the boat's main engine to turn a large impeller that will pump if water gets near the top of the oil pan. The more typical emergency pump is a reliable, gasoline-powered, 200-plus-gallon-per-minute standalone pump. Of course you must be sure it is in working order and that you have the proper type of fuel onboard.

The Captain should be aware of the condition of his or her bilge dewatering system. It should be tested frequently and any problems fixed.

Above Water Leaks – Rain

Two situations come to mind. I once had a leaky out drive boot with my boat on a mooring. I didn't notice the problem until I just happened to look out and see the water streaming from the bilge system. I thought to myself, *where did all that water come from?* I continued to watch. After a couple of minutes, the bilge pump came on again. If I had left the boat in the water, unconnected to shore power, it would have sunk before I came back the next weekend.

I also faced a similar situation with another boat. This boat was also on a mooring. I returned to the boat after a week. The first thing I always do is manually turn on the bilge pump, and usually there is some water in the bilge from either rain or whatever small leak there might be. This time, however, there was no water. I looked in the bilge, and sure enough there was water. *Why wasn't the bilge pump pumping?* I wondered. I checked the voltage of the bilge battery… 0 Volts. I pulled out my trusty spare battery pack and put it on the battery, and sure enough the bilge pump started working and pumped out all the water in the bilge. The problem was it kept going even after all the water was pumped out. The float switch was "stuck on" and wore down the battery. Redundant pumps with redundant batteries are the solution to this problem. Fortunately, there wasn't a large rainstorm that week. What would have happened if I hadn't checked back for 3 weeks and there had been heavy rains? Always consider the possibilities and act accordingly.

Everything fails eventually. Bilge pumps are cheap plastic pumps that at best provide the advertised pumping capacity when they don't have to pump uphill. Bilge pumps fail. You need redundancy here.

Adding Bilge System Strength

At a minimum, every boat and every compartment in a boat should have redundant pumping systems, configured with a primary/backup arrangement and tested regularly. Every boat should also have a high water alarm system and an indicator that tells the owner and the captain that the pump has been running constantly for a period of time. Table 9 indicates a nominal amount of pumping per boat length. It is just a guide. You cannot have too much pumping capacity.

Table 9: Bilge Pump Sizing

Boat Length	No. Pumps	Total Capacity - GPH
16–20	2	5000
21–26	2	6000–6500
27–35	3	7500–8500
36–42	3	9000
43–49	3–4	10000
50–59	4–5	11000–12,000
60 –+	4–5	12,000+

Bilge Pump Installation

At least one high water alarm should be installed to give early warning of a large leak.

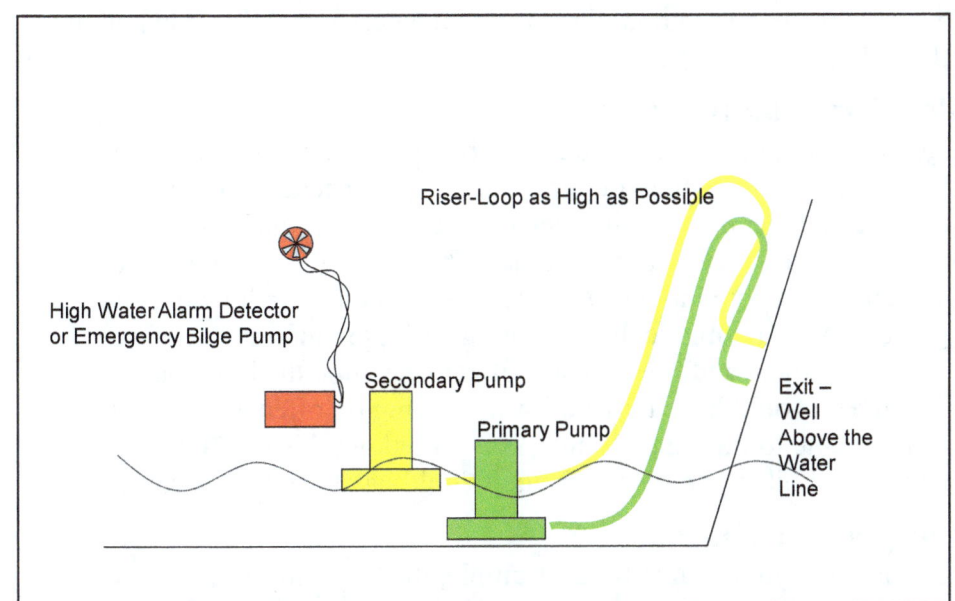

Figure 14: Bilge System Placement

Bilge Pump Switch

There are several different types of automatic bilge pump switches. Each type has its problems, but all of them are adequate if you take proper care in installing and maintaining them. All bilge pump switches are wired and, therefore, require proper wiring—neat, protected, and properly sized.

High Water Alarm

I read about a 30-something-foot boat last summer that sunk close to shore. The Captain said he heard a thump but didn't think much of it at first. A short while later, he went below for something else and noticed water on the floor. It was above the lower deck and rising. This is not the ideal way to find out you are sinking. You should have some type of monitor or high water alarm that would indicate high water or a large leak. This type of monitoring provides precious time to prepare for an emergency.

High water alarms are simply an audible indication connected to a float or other type of switch that goes off when the bilge water rises over a certain level. That level should be well below the cabin floor. In addition, it is always a good idea to add an emergency bilge pump along with the high water alarm.

Bilge Pump Monitoring

Bilge monitors tell you when the bilge pumps have been on for more time than usual, indicating a large leak. Another friend of mine had a slow but steady leak in his shift cable boot. I noticed the bilge pump coming on once every 3 minutes or so. The operator of the boat had no idea there was a potential problem because he had no indications the bilge pump was automatically activating. A bilge pump monitor would have given him an audible or visual alert every time the bilge pump came on. He would have noticed it was coming on often and he would have been able to fix the problem. As it turned out, his boat kept afloat due to a good bilge pump system but it could have been disastrous.

Emergency Pumps

In the previous high water alarm example, the boat didn't have adequate bilge pumping in case of an emergency. The only thing the Captain could do was maneuver to shallow water, get everyone in life jackets, and abandon ship. Had the boat been equipped with an emergency pump, he could have maneuvered to a marina where his boat could have been hoisted ashore and the problem fixed with no collateral damage. As it was, however, the boat went under, which experts indicate will cost

40% of the original price of the boat to fix. How much would an emergency pump have cost?

To review:

- At a minimum, have enough bilge pump capacity to overcome a complete failure of your largest through hull fitting or drain plug. We cannot specify a capacity that will be enough for any situation. The more capacity you have, the less chance you will have of sinking. You must trade off the cost vs. capability.
- Inspect and test your bilge system often. Include float switch, wiring, junk in the bilge, etc.
- At a minimum, use 2 completely separate redundant bilge pump systems.
- Always have a high water bilge alarm. Redundancy here would also be good.
- Have bilge system monitoring, which provides an indication that something is wrong in the bilge faster that your standard high water alarm.
- Have emergency gasoline-powered pumps.

Thunder & Lightning Storms

Lightning is unpredictable. It can blow holes in your hull, start fires, damage or destroy electronics, and, worst case scenario, kill you. While we cannot guarantee that neither you or your boat will be struck by lightning, you can decrease the likelihood that you and your boat will be damaged.

Thunderstorms

Thunder and lightning are so ubiquitous, and even normal, sometimes they seem harmless. Although somewhat rare, people and boats can and do get stuck by lightning regularly. According to Ewen Thompson [33], in Southwest Florida perhaps 3% of sailboats are struck by lightning while moored each year. The Captain of a small craft needs to protect his or her boat and passengers from this insidious form of damage. Even with the best preparation, however, no one can absolutely guarantee safety because lightning is so unpredictable.

The number-one way to reduce the risk of lightning damage to life and property is to avoid thunderstorms. A good rule of thumb is, "If you can hear thunder, even distant thunder, then you may get hit by lightning."

If you have heard the old adage that lightning never strikes the same place twice, forget about it. There have been several documented cases where the same boat was struck multiple times. One sailboat received two lightning strikes within 10 seconds of one another while sailing in the Indian Ocean.

Anyone who gets hit by lightning usually dies. A properly designed boat that gets hit, on the other hand, usually receives minimal damage. The skipper needs to know that his boat is protected, how to protect life aboard, and when to be concerned about lightning.

Rule #1 Avoid Thunderstorms: Certain techniques can be used to recognize and track approaching thunderstorms. Recognizing cumulonimbus clouds is helpful in identifying a thunderstorm. These clouds can be recognized by their cotton puff-like appearance. As the storm progresses, the first few lightning strikes are in the clouds. While they often cannot be seen, they can be detected by turning on an AM radio, whether or not it is tuned to a particular station. Lightning will produce a crackle or static that can be heard and interpreted as a lightning strike. Sometimes lightning from 100 miles away will produce static in the AM band. With practice, however, you will be able to discern loud static as locally present lightning.

As the lightning begins to hit the ground, you will be able to see it and locate the direction it's coming from. Once you locate the direction, you can track it with a handheld compass. If the direction remains about the same and seems to be getting closer, the storm is heading your way. If it seems to be getting farther away, you can relax because it is going away from you. As you keep tracking the direction, you also can track the distance by counting the seconds between lightning and thunder. Every 5 seconds equals about one mile. Keep in mind that a typical thunderstorm is 10 miles high and ten miles across; therefore, you can count up to 50 for a lightning strike at the opposite edge of the storm. A good rule of thumb is, "If you can hear thunder, the storm is close enough to hit you where you are."

Signs of impending lightning strikes include St Elmo's fire, buzzing radio antennas, or wire stays. If you experience any of these, electrical charges are building in your immediate vicinity and you should prepare for an immediate lightning strike.

Lightning

Lightning is caused by opposite charges building until the electrons jump from the negative charge to the positive charge. Actually, the lightning moves from the negative to the positive until the last part of the journey in which the positive side jumps to reach the negative part. This last positive to negative jump is only the last 30 or 100 yards of the lightning bolt. Negative and positive charges build up in the clouds. Whenever the discharge occurs in the clouds, it is not dangerous to life or property on the ground or in the water.

Sometimes, however, the negative charge discharges to the positively charged earth (or water). This is the ground strike that causes damage here on earth. The loud noise heard as thunder comes from the area in the lightning channel. The temperature becomes 6 times hotter than the sun and literally explodes. The thunder seems to last longer that the actual lightning because sound is generated along the entire lightning channel, and each part of that sound travels to our ears at the same speed of about 600 knots. Sound from the portion of the thunder that's farther away takes longer to reach us and, therefore, makes the sound seem longer.

Attachment

As mentioned earlier, the final part of the lightning bolt, the part that touches the earth, is traveling toward the clouds. The point at which this comes is called the attachment point. We can design a lightning protection system where the attachment point is purposely created with a direct path to the ground (or water).

Side flashes

If the lightning attaches firmly with the ground all of the energy is dissipated into the ground (or water). However, if there is some resistance in the path, the energy will get to the ground in any way it can. Sometimes it jumps to the side and down an alternate path. Anything in this path will be damaged accordingly. It is therefore imperative that the lightning path has low impedance between the point of attachment and the ground.

Grounding System

There are two aspects of a properly designed lightning grounding system: the lightning ground path and the bonding system. The ground path provides a safe way for the lightning to travel from the attachment point to its dispersal in the water. The bonding system connects all large metal objects and reduces the possibility of large voltages developing between large conducting objects. This is important because you might be between the two large conducting objects.

According to ABYC, the USCG and the NFPA, a boat should have an electrical path to discharge lightning from the highest point feasible to a ground plate of at least one square foot below and into the water. The conducting path must have the equivalent electrical carrying capacity of #8 copper wire. A boat so equipped is supposed to provide a cone of protection that extends 90 degrees from the top of the highest conducting point.

Although this has been the conventional wisdom regarding lightning protection for many years, Ewen Thompson has shown that major aspects of the standard are inaccurate, namely: 1) #8 copper wire is not fully adequate to dissipate the heat generated by a high-energy lightning strike, 2) a 1-square-foot ground plane is not large enough to prevent side flashes in fresh water. Thompson has also shown it is exceedingly difficult to fully protect electronic systems from damage from the surges produced by the magnetic flux, which are produced by a lightning strike.

Thompson's research drew the following conclusions: 1) #4 copper wire should be used to carry the current of a lightning strike from the highest point to the ground plane, and 2) Even though a 1-square-foot ground plate is adequate for salt water, there is no adequate solution for lightning protection is fresh water. Additionally, the 90-degree cone of protection that has been repeated for many years is not accurate and is more adequately represented by a 150-foot rolling ball [UL96a].

The grounding plate for a boat in fresh water is not as effective as it is in salt water and requires additional consideration. An aluminum or copper strip placed in line of the boat from bow to stern below the water provides a better ground plate than a 1-square-foot copper plate. Even with this, the ground path will have a higher impedance and will, therefore, be less reliable than the saltwater lightning protection system.

While traveling in fresh water, it is more imperative to avoid a thunderstorm.

Bonding System

If left unconnected, separate metal objects in the vicinity of the lightning path could create potential for large and dangerous voltage. If all these objects are connected by a substantial wire, however, they will all be at the same potential and, therefore, harmless. The bonding system is created to this end.

Connect all metal objects using #8 copper wires. Then connect the entire network of bonding wires to the grounding plate. If not done correctly, onboard shocks could result, which might be fatal to the crew.

Risk to Onboard Life

No matter what kind of onboard protection you have, however, stay away from large metal objects, stay well above the waterline and out of the water…and Pray to God. Lightning is dangerous even in the best-protected boat. In fresh water, it is worse than saltwater.

Risk to Onboard Electronics

Electronic manufacturers don't provide protection against lightning strikes. The boat owner is, therefore, responsible for lightning protection.

A boat owner or skipper can do several things to help protect electronics; even still, there are no guarantees:

- Install transient protection at the power input of each device.
- Twist the wires and place them together in harnesses.
- Place electronics inside metal boxes that are connected to the bonding system.

These precautions will reduce the likelihood of damage, but they are not fool proof. An even better method of protection is to disconnect all wires in and out of electronic devices. Of course, if required for an emergency, they will not be as easily available. This is a decision the skipper needs to make.

Risk to the Hull

Often if your boat is not properly outfitted, the lightning path is to the through hull transducers like a knot meter or bottom sounder. This can cause the transducer to be blown out of the bottom of the hull, leaving a large hole in its place. Other types of holes can be burned in the fiberglass, which can often cause the boat to sink.

Lightning Review
- With lightning there is no guarantee, just better probability.
- In a lightning storm, larger protected boats are safer than smaller protected boats.
- Lightning protection in freshwater is not as effective as it is in salt water.
- The only thing worse than an unprotected sailboat in freshwater is a small unprotected boat without a mast in freshwater. Many deaths occur each year because of lightning strikes in open boats, while few die each year due to lightning strikes in sailboats.
- Even if you are in a small unprotected boat in the middle of a lightning storm, getting into the water is more dangerous than staying in an unprotected boat. Try to stay dry and stay in the center of the boat.

Table 10: Lightning – What to do

Your Goals During a Lightning Storm	What You Can Do
Stay away from lightning and thunder if you can.	Track the storm and stay as far away as possible.
Provide a robust path for the lightning to take that will not damage the hull.	Grounding. This works better in salt water than freshwater
Protect people from stray current.	Bonding. Connect all large metal objects and send them to ground.
Protect electronics from the effects of voltage spikes caused by stray current.	Use twisted pair shielded and grounded power cables, install "Transient Suppressors," and unplug electronic devices during lightning.

Lightning Recommendations
- Stay away from storms, especially while in fresh water.
    - Track impending storms.
- Install and maintain a properly designed lightning ground path.
- Install and maintain a bonding system between all large metal objects onboard.
- Protect electronic devices.

- o Install transient protection on all power connections.
- o Install all wires in twisted pairs include at least one ground
- o Install electronic equipment inside bonded metal containers.
- Protect life
  - o Stay away from metal.
  - o Stay well above the waterline.
  - o Never get in the water.

Chapter 7: Monitoring

A friend of a friend bought a used boat. It was fast, it was flashy, and it had twin engines. He was a happy person. The first week he owned it, he took it off shore many miles and one of the engines quit. Fortunately, the twin engines were able to get him home. Unfortunately, when he got back to shore and to his mechanic, he discovered he had overheated and ruined the port engine.

As it turned out, the engine that overheated was in good condition when it died, though the raw water-cooling pump had failed. Having twin engines masked the problem until the engine became so hot it was fried. This type of failure is frequent, expensive, inconvenient—and preventable.

Not paying attention to the gauges and not having full temperature and flow monitoring, he ran the engine to failure. This type of failure requires monitoring and an alarm. Something that hits you over the head well before the engine overheats would be preferable. The first indication of this type of failure would be a reduction of cooling water flow, the second would be rising exhaust temperature, and the third would be cylinder head over temperature. This person had the latter with no alarm. Proper monitoring and alarming would have saved his engine along with the rest of his boating season.

Last spring I read an article in the newspaper about a man who brought his 42-foot cruiser up to the intercostals waterway from Baltimore, just as he had done many years before. That year was typical, he was well provisioned and well within safety margins, and he knew exactly where he was going and when he would arrive at each port. The story stated he heard a bump in the hull, but ignored it, thinking he'd just hit a piece of debris in the water. After a while, however, the boat began to act sluggishly, so he decided to investigate. His last step onto the lower deck was wet. Turned out the entire lower deck was flooded with about

6 inches of water, which also meant he had a couple of feet of water in the bilge. He managed to maneuver the boat to shallower water, but the boat sank shortly afterward. The accompanying picture was sad.

Upon further inspection, he discovered he'd hit something that created a hole in the hull that allowed water to fill the bilge. Since he had no bilge pump monitor or high water alarm to provide an early warning, his first hard indication of a large leak was sluggish handling. The actual verification of the leak was not a sensor or alarm but his foot submerged in the flooded lower deck.

When the possibility of sinking occurs, you need as much advanced notice as possible. A high water alarm or bilge pump monitor would have provided an alarm.

These are just 2 real-life example of where monitoring would have provided advanced warning of impending emergencies. In the case of the overheated engine, a simple exhaust temperature gauge with an alarm would have given sufficient warning to save the operator's engine. A simple high-water alarm would have alerted him of the sinking cruiser and possibly allowed adequate time to get to shore or perhaps set up an emergency dewatering pump.

Table 11 shows sensors and alarms that are available on the market. The boat owner should seriously consider all the possibilities for failure and be able to recognize a potential failure before damage occurs.

Table 11: Monitoring Sensors

	Cooling	Lube	Fuel	Electrical	Operation	Bilge	Alarm
Oil temp.	x	x					
Cyl head temp.	x						x
Exhaust Manifold surface temp	x						
Exhaust Riser surface temp	x						
Exhaust gas temp.	x						x

	1	2	3	4	5	6	7
Before heat exchanger temp.	x						
After heat exchanger temp.	x						
Raw water side input temp.	x						
Raw water side output temp.	x						
Engine coolant flow	x						x
Raw water cooling flow rate	x						x
Oil pressure		x					x
Oil filter clogging indicator		x					x
Water in oil		x					x
Fuel pressure			x				x
Fuel flow rate			x		x		
Fuel level			x		x		x
Water in fuel			x				x
Amperage				x			x
Voltage				x			x
RPM					x		
GPS speed					x		
Water speed					x		
Bilge pump count or amount						x	
Bilge pump flow						x	
High water						x	x

Bilge Monitoring

The example in the introduction of this chapter gives adequate reasons for bilge system monitoring. Simple, inexpensive, reliable sensors are readily available to alert the operator of an impending emergency.

High Water Alarm

Every boat larger than a rowboat should have a high water alarm in every separated compartment. They are simple, reliable, and provide advanced warning of an impending disaster. At least two types of high water alarms are on the market. The simplest is a float switch. This type is effective as long as it remains clear of obstructions and the wiring is secure. The second type is electronic. Two probes measure electrical property changes when both probes become submerged. This type is perhaps the most reliable since debris cannot obstruct its operation.

Whichever type of high water sensor you use, it generally invokes a visible and audible alarm. That alarm must be loud enough for the operator to hear over the din of the engines. Test the high water senor and alarm system regularly to ensure proper operation.

Bilge Pump Monitor

There are multiple types of bilge monitors:

- Bilge pump running too long – indicates when the pump has been on for a long period, nominally 2 minutes. This will provide the first alert when something is wrong in the bilge. Either there is a large leak or the bilge pump is not operating properly.
- Bilge pump running with no flow – indicates the pump is on (either manually or with a float switch) but that no water is exiting. In other words, something is wrong that you must deal with. Many things can go wrong in a bilge pump system: the manual switch may have been left on, the line may be clogged, the pump may be frozen or clogged, etc. This type of monitor provides a status for the condition of the dewatering system.
- Count of bilge pump activations – indicates a simple count of the number of bilge pump activations since reset. This will provide an indication of the amount of water leaking into the bilge over time. Watching this value will tell you if something on your boat is causing an increased leak.
- Percentage of time the bilge pump was on over various periods – provides the most accurate indication of how much water the boat is taking on over time.

Water in the Fuel

Water can enter the fuel system in several ways. Moisture can enter the fuel by condensation in the fuel tank, via contaminated fuel, or via an improperly installed tank vent. However it enters, you want to make sure you get it removed as soon as possible. This requires you to know that you have water in the fuel. Water-in-the-fuel sensors are available for diesel fuel and for gasoline outboard motors. Unfortunately, there is no sensor available for gasoline inboard engines. When possible, however, sensors that tell you that you have water in your fuel should be mandatory for all engines.

If allowed to sit for long periods, diesel fuel develops some type of biological matter, usually referred to as sludge and slime, a condition that accelerates with heat and water. There are methods for getting rid of water in the tank but you will only use these methods if you have evidence of water in the fuel.

Fuel Level Monitoring

I talk to a surprising number of people who have run out of fuel because they didn't have an adequate fuel gauge. My grandfather's 1957 Chris-Craft came with a mahogany stick, which, when inserted into the gas tank, reliably showed the level of the gas. Although inconvenient, it was a reliable method. As boats became more sophisticated, however, manufacturers added dash-mounted fuel level monitors that are slightly less reliable.

Unless you actually run out of fuel, you will never really know how far down the gauge goes when you are out of fuel. Does it go to "E" and still have 10 gallons? Does it register 1/8 of a tank when you have zero fuel? The only real way to be sure is to run out of fuel on purpose. Obviously, you plan this on a nice calm day with good weather, with good batteries, and with an extra amount of fuel to easily take you back to the fuel dock.

If possible, fashion a mahogany stick, just in case.

Engine Condition Monitoring

Engine monitoring and alarms are critical to reducing major damage by identifying loss of critical capabilities such as cooling and lube.

Engine Temperature Monitoring

Engine temperature cannot be completely determined from one sensor and one gauge. Most sensors that come on a factory engine measure the water temperature at one of the cylinder heads. While many times this is enough, more detail will likely provide a quicker alert and less potential damage to the engine.

One potential problem is false readings. If there is no water in the cylinder head, you will get a false low temperature reading because there is no water to measure. The cylinder head is the last place that gets hot. When the cylinder head gets hot, you have a problem. You would rather detect an over-temperature before the cylinder head gets over-temp. Sensing exhaust temperature or cooling water flow is a better place to detect cooling system problems.

For raw water cooling problems, the exhaust manifold is the first place to check for over-temperature. The surface of the exhaust manifold and riser should be lower than $140°F$. In some cases it might be $150°F$, but never $160°F$. An electronic, mechanical, or chemical monitor can provide early warning of cooling problems. The simplest, most reliable monitor is the chemical temperature strip. When mounted on the clean surface of the exhaust manifold, it will permanently change color if the temperature exceeds the rated value. Stick it on and check it at the end of the day. The surface temperature of the exhaust manifold will show an increase well before the engine overheats.

All marine engines with cooled exhaust should have an exhaust temperature probe on each exhaust manifold. When operating properly, this temperature will be less than 200 degrees F. A rise in exhaust temperature will be the first indication of a raw water-cooling restriction.

In some marine engines, a closed cooling fluid circuit is directly cooling the engine with a separate raw water circuit cooling the cooling fluid via heat exchanger. Other types of systems cool the engine directly with raw cooling water. Different circumstances warrant different sensor configurations.

In a closed circuit configuration, for example, two sensors are required to isolate a thermostat failure. The thermostat will restrict the closed circuit coolant until the temperature increases; that will cause the thermostat to allow coolant to flow. If there is a sensor on the hot side of the raw cooling water as well as on the closed circuit side, a bad thermostat will show up as an overheated cylinder head and a cool raw water output.

Low flow of the raw water pump will show up first as an increased output temperature of the raw water and an increased temperature in the exhaust probe.

Watch for these situations over multiple hours or days. It is important to know what is normal so you can detect an abnormal trend.

To increase your knowledge of the cooling system, Figure 15 shows where multiple sensors may be placed.

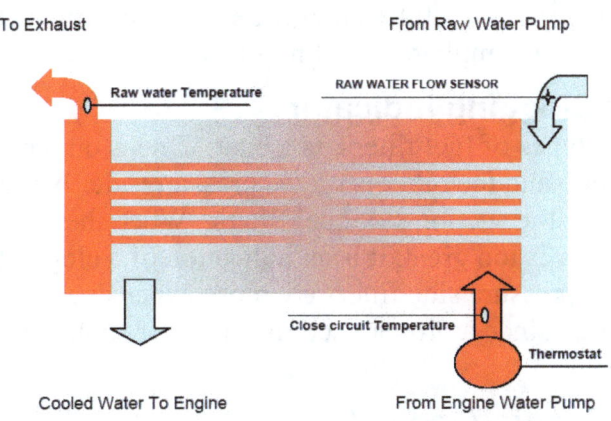

Figure 15: Closed Circuit Cooling

Raw Water Flow Monitoring

The introduction to this chapter described a new owner who ran his boat to overheating and engine ruination because he did not know whether adequate cooling water was reaching the engine. Simple flow indicators are available, however, to reveal this issue. A non-flow restricting device is better than a device that restricts the flow. This latter type might become the problem if it impedes the flow even the slightest bit.

Engine Oil Pressure

A close acquaintance of mine knows nothing about engines. His first car developed a lighting problem. A stupid little red light would come on, which made it hard to see at night. He solved the problem by putting a band-aid over the light. After a couple of days, the lighting problem was solved because the engine seized up. The light he covered was the low oil pressure light. All engines should have an oil pressure gauge with a visual and audible alarm that alerts the operator to turn off the engine and fill it with oil.

Filter Clogging Indicators

Filters sometimes clog, and sometimes mechanics change them too often. When they become fully clogged, engine performance suffers and sometimes cause a complete loss of mobility.

Fuel Filter Clogging Indicator

There are two types of fuel filters on a boat. One is on the vacuum side of the fuel pump and the other is on the pressure side. Vacuum gauges are available for the suction side fuel filters. When the vacuum on the input to the filter is too great, it is an indication of a clogged filter. Filter monitoring for pressure side filters are more expensive and should not even be required since a proper suction side filter should always be the main filter.

Oil Filter Clogging Indicator

Since the oil filter is under pressure on both sides, you cannot use a single vacuum gauge to determine the clogging level. Instead, a differential pressure gauge is required, which indicates the difference between the pressure on one side of the filter and the pressure on the other side. Even though these are available commercially, they should be even more widely available and used more often.

Air Filter Clogging Indicator

It is important not to change the air filter before it is necessary. An SAE study determined an engine would last up to 60% longer if the air filter were allowed to work to its maximum. This is because an air filter becomes more efficient as it becomes clogged. Of course, a tradeoff is made between having enough air and having enough efficiency.

Like the fuel filter, a single vacuum gauge provides monitoring of the air filter. The system measures the vacuum on the clean side of the filter. You change the filter when the magnitude of the vacuum reaches a certain point.

Battery Charge and Condition

Keeping track of the condition of battery will keep you from being stranded. Both the amount of the charge (voltage) and the ability to hold a charge (amperage) should be considered. Just because a battery's voltage is 12V, that does not mean it can hold a charge or do any particular amount of work.

One way to determine the condition of a battery is to measure the voltage while the battery in under load. There are special devices on the market for this, but you may also measure the voltage on your own while the engine is starting. Keep a log regarding the voltage during start from the time the battery is new until it is ready to be replaced. You will then have an excellent record that will provide you with knowledge of your battery condition.

Navigation Monitoring

Redundant electronic navigation monitoring is available today at reasonable prices. Never rely on one device, especially some of the earlier GPS units. Early GPS units just stop working if the internal battery fails, without any warning or recourse. This usually means sending the unit back to the manufacturer and replacing the $3.00 battery with a $50 one. This is not only irritating, but it could also mean loss of navigation monitoring when you need it most. Always operate a backup with a breadcrumb trail so you can at least get back home.

As convenient, inexpensive, and easy to use as a GPS/Loran navigation unit is, you should always have a manual backup. Your most reliable method of navigating is paper charts and aids to navigation. Have these available to track yourself on a paper chart.

Chapter 8: Emergency Planning

What Happens in an Emergency

On May 27, 1977, a Pan Am Boeing 747 was struck by a KLM Jet as it rushed out of the fog at 160 MPH, which tore the top off the Pan Am jet. Floy Heck, her husband, and a few friends were on that plane. When the collision occurred, she could not speak or move. According to her recollection, "My mind was almost blank. I didn't even hear what was going on." Her husband, on the other hand, immediately jumped up and ordered her to get off the plane. As they jumped out onto the emergency shoot, Floy looked back and saw her friend just sitting there calmly with her hands folded, looking straight ahead. Like dozens of others, her friend died in the flames that engulfed the jet shortly thereafter. So while Floy's reaction was to do nothing, her husband's reaction was to get out.

How will you and your passengers act in an emergency? Your boat catches fire, starts sinking, or someone falls overboard. According to a *Time Magazine* article [31], about 10-15% of you will remain calm and act quickly, another 15% or so will lose it and freak out, while the majority of you will do little except be "stunned and bewildered."

One striking fact that NIST found during a study of the 911 Twin Towers disaster was that the average person took 6 minutes to decide to evacuate the building. Some people took a lot longer, lingering for a half hour before deciding to leave. A surprising number of people turned off their computers before leaving or met in a conference room to make a joint decision to leave.

The problem here is that our brains do not respond well to unfamiliar scenarios. It takes us 10 seconds to respond to each new piece of information as we search for the best way out of a bizarre problem. With hundreds of new pieces of information to digest and resolve, several minutes can expire without any progress toward increasing our chances for survival. This time can mean the difference between continued existence and the alternative.

Floy Heck's husband did something unusual before their plane was hit by the KLM flight. He pulled out the emergency pamphlet, read it, and looked around for the nearest emergency exit. He was planning for the worst even though he did not expect it. As a result, the information was right at the top of his memory stack in case of an emergency. He responded quickly because he did not have to think. He just reacted to the plan he had readily stored in his brain. Ever since Mr. Heck was caught in a theater fire as a boy, he has always had an escape route planned no matter where he is.

Similarly, Manuel Chea did everything right while on the 49th floor of Tower 1 of the World Trade Center on 9/11/2001. When asked why he responded quickly and calmly, he responded with several theories. In previous years, he had escaped from his burning house while he was blinded by the smoke. When he was a child, he was in a serious earthquake in Peru, and later in life he suffered through several earthquakes in Los Angeles. Like Mr. Heck, he, too, was prepared for action simply by having an escape plan worked out in his mind.

So what does this mean to us? We need to have a plan, we need it to be as simple and as effective as possible, we need it committed to memory, and we need to let our passengers know what is expected of them. We need a plan for fire, sinking, and man overboard (MOB) because seconds count. There is no time to think about the problem; there is only time to execute a plan. So plan an escape route in case of an emergency before you get on the boat.

Plan

Planning is part of boating that is often done only after you have experienced the discomfort of a near disaster. For example, I always plot the course before taking off if I am going to an unknown area. I do this because I once hit ground while not paying attention to where I was and where I was going. This happened even though my GPS chart plotter clearly showed the shoal that I hit. If you plot first, you will eliminate this type of stupid mistake.

That goes for any trips. The better you prepare the better you will be able to handle what comes your way. Besides fire, flood, and man overboard (MOB), you need a plan for what you do if:

- you run low on fuel
- your engine won't start
- you get caught in a storm
- someone aboard gets sick or is injured
- the skipper becomes incapacitated and someone needs to take over

While this is by no means an exhaustive list of all the things you need to think about in the event of an emergency, it will get you thinking about planning for the good as well as the bad.

Identify a First Mate

The most important redundancy you can bring aboard is a redundant skipper. If you are fortunate to have a spouse who can take over, that is great. If you do not, you need to bring one of your passengers up to speed about emergency equipment and procedures. The first mate should also know how to maneuver the boat and find his or her way home.

Plan for Rough Weather

As we discussed earlier, the *Questar* [28] was a small boat operating in rough weather without the aid of a VHF radio, proper bilge pumps, or water/fuel separation and detection. First of all, this was a small open bow fishing boat that had no business being out with a small craft advisory in effect. The boat had a small bilge pump that was not able to keep up with the water coming onboard, so the passenger had to manually bail out the hull and was still unable to keep up with the water coming onboard.

If you do any type of boating, chances are you will be out in bad weather at some point. Storms can come up fast. Waves from distant storms can come seemingly out of nowhere.

Always carry a sea anchor. If all else fails, you can throw the sea anchor out to hold the bow into the wind and waves. It will keep your drifting to a minimum and keep you afloat until the storm dies down.

Carry foul weather gear for the Captain and the crew. A cold, wet day is far worse than a cold, dry day. Wool does its job even when it gets wet, so bring wool sweaters instead of plastic ones.

Minimum Supplies and Equipment

Make sure you have the right set of equipment and supplies onboard. Steven Callahan documented his 76 days at sea in a life raft in his book *Adrift* [32] and had more lines of different sizes than I could ever imagine needing. For some reason he brought them aboard his life raft before his boat sank. Nonetheless, the book goes on to explain how useful every tool and every piece of line was to keeping him and his life raft afloat. If you haven't read it, you should.

is a starting point for your checklist of things to bring aboard. Depending on where you are going, who you are going with, what type of boat you are going on, etc., you may need all kinds of things. So use a checklist like this one and update it on every voyage.

Emergency Repair

Figure 16 depicts the use of the collision mat is made from some sort of fabric with useful ties on each corner. It is usually more effective to fill a temporary hole from the outside than from the inside. If you ever need it you will be glad to have it.

Similarly, bungs can be useful in extreme cases to plug leaks in through hull fittings in an emergency (see Figure 17). They can be made of wood or plastic. The right size is critical here. If you need them you will be glad to have them.

Leak Repair

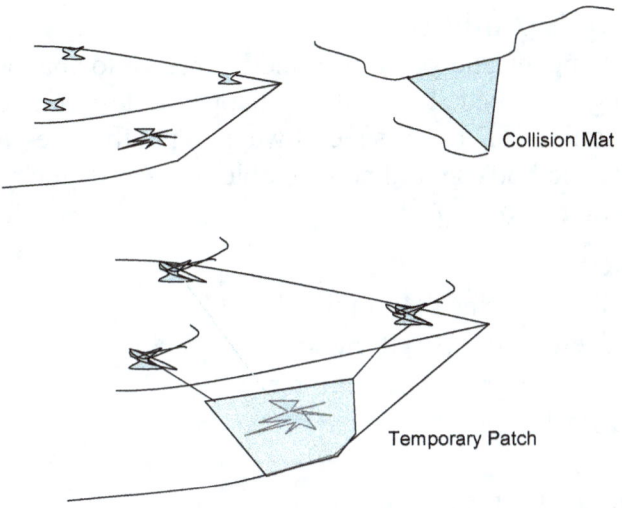

Figure 16: Collision Mats

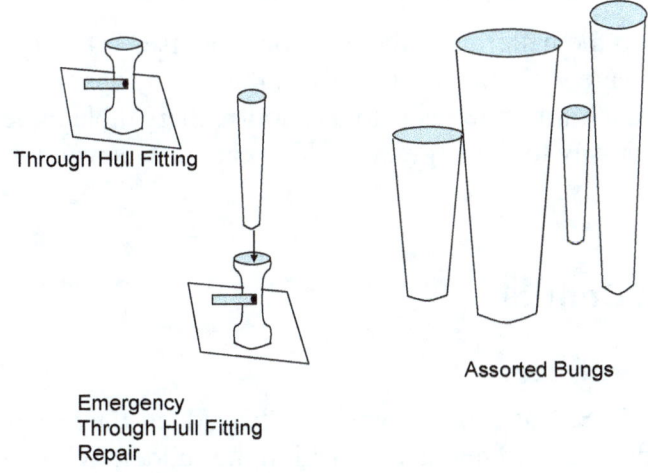

Figure 17: Bungs

Emergency Signaling

If the worst happens and you are stranded or have to abandon ship, you will want to get rescued. That will not happen unless someone knows you need rescuing. There are several ways to get that message across to others. These methods should be available in an emergency and even in a separate waterproof bag:

- EPIRB
- Handheld marine VHF radio
- Handheld aircraft VHF radio
- High power green laser pointer
- LED flashlight
- Flares
- Batteries for the above

If you've ever read stories about people lost at sea, one thing stick out in most of them. They usually come close to a ship or see an aircraft but cannot signal them. This has got to be heart breaking. Ships and aircraft are required to monitor emergency channels when at sea. All you have to do is call them… if you have the proper radio.

Don't keep the batteries in the electronic devises. They can leak and cause damage without warning. Keep them in a separate baggie. The best approach for batteries is to use non-rechargeable batteries unless you have a way to recharge them. You can carry several sets of alkaline batteries easily

Loss of Control

Loss of Rudder:

When the U.S. Navy loses control of the rudder, they send a team down to the rudder area to manually position the rudder. While this may or may not be possible in your boat, you can steer enough to get home by dragging a bucket or drogue out the stern. Move it to port to turn port and move it to starboard to turn starboard. Once you're heading in the proper direction, you will need less steering. Make sure your rudder is in the straight position to minimize your bucket maneuvering.

Loss of Stern Drive Steering:

Steering cables go bad, particularly when you least want them to. I know; it's happened to me. My solution was to tie 2 lines on the farthest extent of the out drive as possible, and then post 2 people—one port and one starboard—to pull the lines and turn the boat. This works ok, but you would not want to do this by yourself.

Steering with One Engine:

The loss of one engine on a twin inboard will many times result in a difficult-to-steer passage. Rudders are sized to reduce drag while still being able to steer with both engines running. If one engine fails, the rudders will normally need to compensate for the drag of the failed side and the offset of the running side. If you have twin screws, try it on a nice day. You will probably find it hard to move in a straight line, let alone be able to maneuver back into a slip.

There are a couple of things you can do to ease this situation. If you drag a water bucket or a sea anchor from the boat on the side with the running engine, (see Figure 18) you will be better able to move in a straight line. Be sure to use a polypropylene line or some other material that will float, and take other measures so the line doesn't get caught in the prop.

Brief bursts of forward and reverse will help you maneuver the stern while easing forward. If you have a right hand screw, reverse will walk the stern slightly to port and forward will walk the stern slightly to starboard. The opposite situation will occur if your running screw is left. A little experimentation will help you determine which side is which. The best approach is to try it on a good day with little congestion around you. Just turn one engine off and try to maneuver with the other.

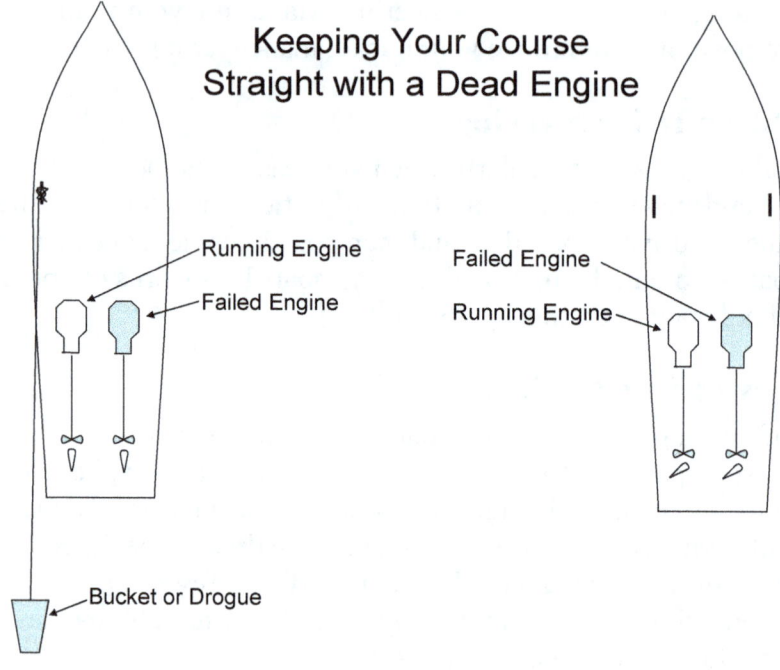

Figure 18: Keep Your Course with a Dead Engine

Damage Control Boards

I suggest making a damage control notebook with a diagram or schematic of all of your vital systems, and possibly even your non-vital systems. The U.S. Navy does this for every system onboard. They diagram every wire, valve, pipe, winch, etc., on one or more of what they call the "damage control boards" and hang them in a large book-like configuration in the damage control room. Each page in the book diagrams a separate system and is about 3 feet by 4 feet in size. Each diagram is made of semi-rigid plastic so those onboard can draw on it with a grease pencil. For the non-military boater, this is probably overkill, but the principle is useful.

Make an easy-to-understand color diagram of each of your vital systems so that you can read them easily when you're under pressure and need them the most. Have the pages laminated so they will be waterproof.

Letter-sized (8.5" X 11") pages will be fine. Keep them in a notebook that can be quickly found and used in emergency situations.

Since you might not be the one doing the emergency repairs, remember to make them easy to understand and use. Labeling the parts might be a good idea, both on your paper and on the boat.

While this simple technique will cost you little, it can potentially get you through an emergency situation.

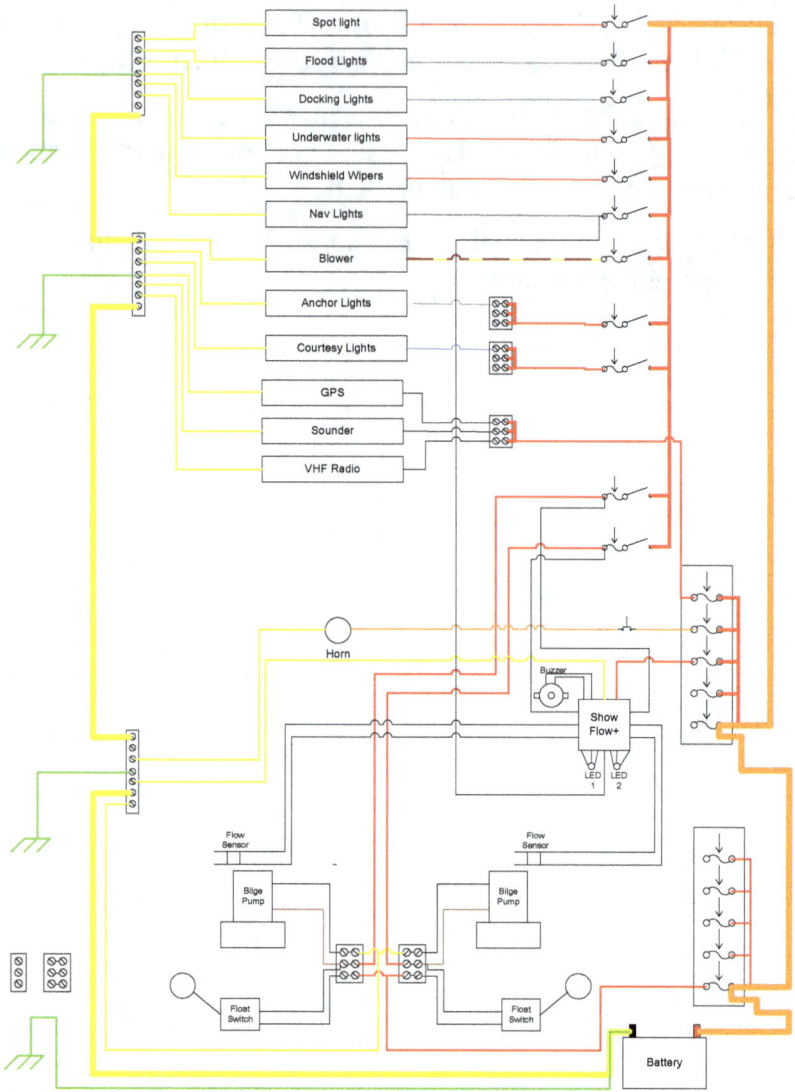

Figure 19: Damage Control Board Example

Running Aground

A U.S. Navy captain automatically loses his command if his ship's hull even touches the bottom, no matter what the reason. One of your highest priorities is to make every effort to stay away from risky and shallow areas. You will encounter them, however, and whether the grounding is due to poor navigation, shifting-sand bottom, or tidal action, you need a plan to get your boat floating again, safely and without damage.

Your first reaction might be to slam the boat in reverse and power yourself off the shoal. If you attempt this without checking the cooling water intake, props, and rudder, however, you will likely bend screws or suck debris into the cooling water, clog things up, and overheat the engine. The resulting damage could be catastrophic.

A better approach would be to stop the engine, examine the situation, and be sure the engine cooling water intake, props, and rudders are free before using the engine. Determine the steps you will take and produce a mental plan of what you can do and in which order.

Also, avoid having a passing powerboat pull you off the shoal. Again, the first reaction is to throw a line, attach it to both respective bitts, and power it off. Most powerboats, however, can provide enough power to pull both sets of bitts out of the two hulls or snap a three-strand nylon rope like a rubber band, which is exactly what it becomes. Nylon lines will stretch 30% or 40% and then snap with tremendous potential energy. If anyone or anything is in line with it when it snaps, you will be amazed at the damage the untamed line will inflict. Again the best approach is to stop and assess the situation, then proceed with a well-thought-out plan.

Some techniques to consider are:

- Lighten the load.
- Initiate a tug-o-war between human and shoal.
- Use a small anchor to apply force in a desired direction, otherwise known as "kedging."
- Use the tide and waves.
- Safely use the power from a passing powerboat.
- Heel over to reduce the draft.

Manually pull using all available passengers. Sometimes it is possible to pull the boat off a sandbar using a tug-o-war approach. I have actually done this, and the more people you have, the better. You can also try rocking the boat with the waves to gain some advantage. After checking the engine water intake, you may be able to use the engine(s) to help. Be sure to check the engine temperature and manifold temperature while the engine is running. The cooling system might be clogged with debris or sand, which can cause overheating.

Kedging is a technique of moving or turning a boat using an anchor set well away from the boat. Use as large a scope as practical, at least 3:1+. With this procedure, you will use a dingy, pfd, fender, or other method to float the anchor away from the boat. Set it in deeper water and use it to try to pull yourself off the shoal using some type of mechanical advantage. Sailboats sometimes have a manual winch to gain a mechanical advantage. The usual anchor chain windless was not designed for this type of work and should be avoided.

Use the tide or waves. Be sure to know the direction and timing of the tide. If it is coming in, you might want to wait for the high tide to float you off. If it is going out and you can't get loose in time, try minimizing the damage by cushioning your hull against the ground as it lays down.

Pulling off with a passing powerboat. As mentioned previously, this technique can be dangerous to both people and property; however, properly done, it can work. The operator of the pulling boat must understand the risks and must not apply too much power. Use a towline that does not stretch before it breaks. Polypropylene and Dacron (polyester) will minimize the potential energy if the line snaps.

Heeling a sailboat with a keel. With a sailboat, you can use the winches, the boom, and the mainsail to your advantage. If the wind is pushing you farther onto the shoal, let down the sail. Try to heel the boat to reduce your draft. Move people to the deep-water side and swing the boom the same way. You may be able to get volunteers to hang on to the end of the boom to further heel the boat. Additionally, you may add some other weight to the end of the boom, like a dingy full of water.

Check for damage. After you are free, examine the bilge to be sure your boat isn't leaking. Also, check the rudder and prop shaft for damage. As mentioned before, check the cooling water intake for debris. As you run the engines, keep an eye on the temperature. A clogged intake will cause overheating.

As a last resort, call a towboat. This requires a properly operating radio or cell phone, so it is important to keep these in good operating condition throughout the ordeal.

I hope one of these techniques will provide the necessary solution to your dilemma with little or no damage to life or property.

Prove It Before You Use It

This section discusses sea trials and testing different systems on your boat, including running out of gas, testing redundant systems, going out in different types of weather, and trying out repairs and new installations before going to sea. You need to gain confidence and improve areas in your boat that need improvement before putting your trust in any part of it. Your life and the lives of your crew may depend on it.

In the introduction of this book, we provided an account of a tragic accident where people were killed. The skipper was an experienced sailor, and his crew was young but experienced. The weather was not the problem. He knew what kind of weather he'd be heading into before he left port. Normally he would have been able to handle the situation, but the problem was he didn't prove the boat and, therefore, didn't know what to expect from it. As a result, it let him down, just as it would according to Murphy's Law.

The boat was new to the skipper, the first time he had sailed her. He didn't know the reliability of anything, and he didn't know the condition of the fuel or the filters. Since he didn't have experience with that particular boat and its particular set of systems, it failed at the worst time (Murphy's Law once again).

He expected to use the engine to keep her in the wind but something went wrong and the engine failed when he needed it most. It is over for him; there is no learning from mistakes. You should only take out an unproven boat in good weather and when you're not in any particular hurry to get anywhere.

Proving your boat should always be done prior to taking an extended trip, preferably while cruising with another boat. I don't want to sound overly dramatic, but every Captain needs to take his or her responsibility seriously when departing from shore with other human beings onboard.

So prove your boat before you use it. Before you take a long cruise with unknown weather or unknown seas, take many small outings on good days in calm seas. It's all about being able to efficiently handle emergency situations with confidence.

Run full throttle for an hour or so. You might not want to waste the fuel right now, but if you ever want to get away from a lightning storm you won't know how well your fuel system works until it's too late. Then if there is a problem with any of the systems on your boat, you will eventually find out. Better to do so when you have more control of the situation.

Try running out of fuel. This might sound stupid, but if you do it while cruising on a nice day with a buddy vessel, while you have spare fuel onboard, and while you're near a fuel station, you will know for sure whether the fuel gauges work and how much battery you will need to re-prime the system.

A friend of mine ran out of gasoline twice in an unproven boat on the same trip. Each time, he limped to the nearest filling station, dutifully cleaned the carburetor filter, thinking that he had a clogged filter. Each time it ran like a champ after the cleaning. After all, it must have been the filter was clogged because the gauge said the tanks were still half full. After paying for 100 gallons of fuel twice, he began to think, how big is this tank? It certainly wasn't 200 gallons as the fuel gauge indicated. Turns out, it was empty. Now he knows the gauge doesn't work and that the tank only holds 100 gallons. This is a good thing to know when you are far from home.

Flood the bilge. Do not get carried away here. I mean run some water into the bilge and let the bilge pump kick in so you can see what it can do. Are all the pumps working automatically? Does the bilge monitor work? Check all bilge subsystems often to be sure they are working.

Take the boat out on a rough day. Who knows? You might find yourself in rough seas with no way out except to get back to shore, but at least you'll be able to handle emergency situations with confidence. Hit some large waves head on. Don't start with a huge one; start with small ones and then progress until you cannot take it anymore. Your boat should be able to take more than you can; otherwise, get a new boat.

If you have just had a repair done or added new equipment to your boat, prove it before you use it. Many times a repair or installation is done improperly and needs to be brought back to the mechanic to re-do it. This is frustrating enough when you are at your slip, but if you are out at sea, it can spell disaster. Remember Murphy's Law: don't trust anything without sufficient proof and testing, especially if a human is in the loop.

Try every piece of equipment you have onboard and expect you might need someday. If you have a sea anchor, battery pack, or search light, try it out. But don't try out the EPIRB. Get used to your VHF radio. If you have a Loran and you don't know how to use it, use it; you might need it someday. Don't wait until you need it to learn how to use it.

Try all of your emergency procedures: Man Overboard (MOB), redundant fuel pump, redundant raw water cooling pump....

If you are never in an emergency or never need to kick in a redundant component, then you are lucky. If you keep cruising the great waterways of this unforgiving world, however, someday you will need the experience gained by proving your boat.

Miscellaneous Reliability Tips

- Incorporate redundancy on critical components. Redundancy is the only way you can reduce the possibility of failure to near zero. The zero percentage here is only for analysis purposes. You can never guarantee anything, but redundancy is the best way to increase your chances of success.
- Do the simple things first. Do not view this book as your opportunity to get rid of your boat just because you cannot do all the things in it. Do what you can, and adjust your boating to the reliability you have achieved. You never want to look stupid. Don't give anyone cause to say, "What? He went 20 miles offshore with only one bilge pump? No wonder it sank. What a jerk." One bilge pump might be adequate for an inland lake where you can get back to your dock in 10 minutes but not if you're 20 miles offshore.

- Use floats on anything important or expensive that might fall overboard and sink. This might seem obvious but things like keys, glasses, wallets (someone should invent a floating wallet), checkbook...
- Keep an emergency credit card, money, and identification onboard in case you lose your wallet. Think about what you would do if you were on a cruise and you lost your wallet. You'd never be able to purchase a ticket to fly home, rent a car, or buy food or fuel. Triple redundancy would be good here.
- Do things to reduce thievery. Placing the name of your boat on your fenders will discourage someone from stealing your fenders (or anything else). In general, things have a lower probability of being stolen if they are inside a container, preferably locked. Keep your expensive stainless-steel barbeque, fenders, boat hooks, PFDs, dock lines, and SS props stowed away. If people can see it and what you have is better then what they have, what you have may be theirs tomorrow.
- Whenever possible, be sure one of your passengers knows how to operate the boat and can get you back to shore in an emergency. Yes, that means husbands must teach their wives to pilot the boat.
- Find out what the safety regulations are and observe them so you can avoid fines and potential catastrophes. PFDs out and available, along with emergency flares that are within reach will work if you need rescue. These safety regulations are just the minimum. Aim for exceeding them.
- Have your prop shaft seals inspected every 6 months. If you notice a gradual increase in the amount of water intake to the bilge, it is probably the prop shaft seals.
- A gasoline vapor sensor can provide you with the needed advanced warning that might save your life or your boat. These simple devices provide an almost instant response when you turn on the ignition. Have them tested periodically. Check with the manufacturer to determine how to best test these devices.
- Monitor how much water is being pumped from your bilge. If you notice an increase, find out where it's coming from and get it fixed ASAP. Monitoring can be done using a simple counter or a sophisticated flow integration device. Even though the flow integration device is much more accurate, the simple counter will provide you with an indication of any increase.
- Do not use automobile parts for your marine engine. Some marine parts, such as the points and condenser, have better protection against moisture. Other marine parts, such as the alternator and the starter motor, are designed not to cause the ignition of fuel vapor in the bilge. Still other engine parts designed for marine use have other safety features. The fuel

pump, for example, will divert a fuel pump leak from the bilge to the intake manifold or carburetor.
- It is a good idea to install a sea water strainer on your raw cooling water intake. I have sucked up all kinds of stuff including a fully intact (but squished) hornet's nest that got stuck in the pump and stopped the flow of raw cooling water to the heat exchanger. Keep in mind the cooling water also cools your exhaust gases. This is a potential fire hazard if the engine exhaust gets too hot.

  Junk stuffed in the cooling line will raise havoc with the cooling of your motor. It is much better to catch the debris before it gets stuck in your pump or clogs up your heat exchanger.

  The strainer is probably best placed before the pump. Be sure to prime the strainer with water after installation and prior to operation. Priming should be done whenever the strainer is emptied or cleaned.

- Don't trust your fuel to a dock attendant. Many attendants are high school or college students getting little more than minimum wage. If they put gasoline in you diesel tank, you are the one who will be stuck with the bill to empty, clean, and refuel the tanks. While a little diesel fuel in with your gasoline isn't bad, a large amount could cause engine damage due to pre-ignition. People make mistakes, but it is up to you to make sure they don't make mistakes on your boat. A label on your fuel filler would be a good safeguard against using the wrong fuel by mistake.
- Take apart, inspect, and lubricate your through hull fittings. If you do not need the fitting, have it removed and the hole repaired. Through hull fittings are a necessary liability, a properly repaired hole in the hull is much more reliable than any through hull fitting.
- A husband and wife were found dead in their engine room [32]. They suffocated because the fire extinguisher activated, eliminating oxygen from the room. Always have an escape route planned and be aware that the fire extinguisher systems are excellent at removing oxygen from the immediate environment.
- Automatic sprinklers, fire detection and alarm systems, and emergency lighting are compulsory on all ships delivered after October 1994 that are able to carry 36 or more passengers [22]. Maybe they should be on your boat

Enjoy

Perhaps we should have put this part at the beginning of the book, but we inserted it last because before you can enjoy, you need to fulfill your obligations as Captain.

I know many people who turn into monsters when they take on the role of Captain.

Bibliography

[1] Fitch, J, 2nd edition, How to Select a Motor Oil and Filter for your Car or Truck. Noria Corporation.

[2] Filtration Technology. 2nd Edition, Bulletin 0247-b1, Parker Hannifin Corp.

[3] J.A McGeehan, P.R. Ryason, "Million Mile Bearings: Lessons From Diesel Engine Bearing Failure Analysis", SAE Paper 1999-01-3576 (1999).

[4] Bruce Kuhnell, "Wear in Rolling Element Bearings and Gears, How age and Contamination Affect Them," Machinery Lubrication Sept – Oct 2004.

[5] Gordon Jones, John Eleftherakis, "Correlating Engine Wear with Filter Multipass Testing," SAE Paper 952555.

[6] Marty Barris, "Total Filtration TM. The Influence of Filter Selection on Engine Wear, Emission, and Performance," SAE Paper 952557.

[7] T. Grafe, MGogins, M Barris, J Schaefer, R, Canepa, "Nanofibers in Filtration Applications in Transportation," Filtration 2001 International Conference and Exposition of the INDA.

[8] Drew Troyer, Jim Fitch, Oil Analysis Basics. Noria Corporation.

[9] David R. Staley, "Correlating Lube Oil Filtration Efficiencies with Engine Wear," SAE Paper 881825.

[10] William M. Needlelman and Puliyur V. Madhavan, "Review of Lubricant Contamination and Diesel Engine Wear," SAE Paper 881827.

[11] Mark J. Beauchamp, "Application of High Efficiency Oil Filtration to Heavy Duty Diesel Bus Engines," SAE Paper 920927.

[12] Brian W. Schwandt and Barry M. Verdegan, "Influence of Lube Oil Filter Performance on Engine Wear in City Buses," SAE Paper 902238.

[13] Drew D. Troyer, How to Lube Up Your FMEA Process, downloaded from www.Noria.com 12/9/2004.

[14] Lube-Tips Newsletter, Noria Corporation, Feb 1, 2005.

[15] Oil Analysis Basics, Noria Inc.

[16] Boating Statistics – 2002, U.S Coast Guard.
[17] Seaworthy Website "Why Boats Sink."
[18] U.S. Coast Guard 2002, Boating Statistics, from the internet.
[19] Seaworthy Magazine Website, "Why Boats Sink."
[20] Seaworthy Magazine Website, "Why Boats Burn,"

[21] Lightning and Sailboats, E,M Thomson, Sea Grant Project No. R/MI-10 Grant # NA89AA-D-SG053, July 1992.

[22] We Are All Safer - NTSB Inspired Improvements in transportation Safety, Pamphlet, 2nd edition, July 1998, National Transportation Safety Board Washington, D.C. 20594

[23] Most Wanted Transportation Safety Improvements - State Issues.

[24] Boating statistics – 2003, U.S. Department of Homeland Security - United States Coast Guard, publication COMDTPUB P16754.17, Oct 2004.

[25] Sinking of the Amphibious Passenger Vehicle Miss Majestic, Lake Hamilton, Near Hot Springs, Arkansas, May 1, 1999, NTSB/MAR-02/01, PB2002-91640 In Marine Accident Report, National Transportation Safety Board, Washington, DC.

[26] National Transportation Safety Board Washington, D.C. 20594 Marine Accident Brief Report PB2001-916402 NTSB/MAR-01/01 Fire On Board The Netherlands Registered Passenger Ship Nieuw Amsterdam Glacier Bay, Alaska May 23, 2000.

[27] Fire On Board the Small Passenger Vessel Port Imperial Manhattan, Hudson River New York City, New York November 17, 2000 NTSB/MAR-02/02 PB2002-916402, Marine Accident Report.

[28] PB96-916402, NTSB/MAR-96/01/SUM

National Transportation Safety Board Washington, D.C. 20594

Marine Accident/Incident Summary Report

Capsizing Of Questar Motorboat And Drowning Of Operator South Of Shelter Island, Near Juneau, Alaska, August 21,1994.

[29] PB99-916401 NTSB/MAR-99/01 National Transportation Safety Board Washington, D.C. 20594 Marine Accident Report Sinking Of The

Recreational Sailing Vessel *Morning Dew* At The Entrance To The Harbor Of Charleston, South Carolina December 29, 1997.

[30] Found on the internet http://www.mcnallyinstitute.com/13-html/13-12.htm 4/22/2005, McNally Institute.

[31] Amanda Ripley, "How to Get Out Alive," Time Magazine, May 2, 2005, pg 58 – 62.

[32] Boating Accidents Of Note To Boaters In Florida's Palm Beaches And Treasure Coast
http://www.geocities.com/palmbeachboating/accidents.html January 2005.

[33] "A Critical Assessment of the U.S. Code for Lightning Protection of Boats," *IEEE Transactions on Electromagnetic Compatibility*, Vol 33, No. 2, May 1991

Appendix
Minimum Supplies and Equipment Checklist

Table 12: Equipment and Supplies Checklist

Supplies and Equipment		Urgency (H,M,L)	Optional	
Tools				
	2 sizes Phillips screwdriver	H		Could use 2 pairs of 4 in 1 screwdriver.
	2 sizes regular screwdriver	H		
	2 sizes adjustable wrench	H		
	Wire cutters	H		
	Pliers	H		
	Pry bar	L	X	
	Vise Grips	H		
	Open end wrenches 3/8" - 7/8" or Metric 7 - 18	H	X	Some boats are metric; some are SAE
	Pocket knife	H		
	2 rugged flashlights	H		
	12 V portable battery pack	M		
	Jumper cables	L		
	Socket wrench set (Metric or SAE)	M	X	Some boats are metric; some are SAE
	Allen wrenches (Metric or SAE)	L	X	Depends if you have allen screws
	Spark plug wrench	M	X	NOT REQUIRED FOR DIESELS

	Spark Monitor	L	X	NOT REQUIRED FOR DIESELS
	Voltage and continuity checker (VOM)	M		
	Insulated clip jumper wires	L		
	Electrical Terminals and tool	L		
	Ignition feeler gauge if points are used	M	X	Depends if you have points
Supplies				
	Extra $	H		
	Extra fuses	H		
	Nylon line small and med	H		
	Tow line	H		
	Extra oil	H		
	WD-40			
	Mechanics wire			20-30 feet of ~18 gauge galvanized steel wire for emergency repairs
	Duct tape	H		
	Extra fuel filters	H		
	Extra air filter(s)	H		
	Black electrical tape	H		
	Spare v-belt or serpentine belt	H		
	Rubber fuel line and clamps	M		
	Wire, multiple gauges	M		
	Spare propeller	H		

Spare ignition parts (points, plugs, condenser ignition coil, distributor cap, and rotor) as equipped	M		
Supplies and Equipment	Urgency (H,M,L)	Optional	
Extra engine thermostat	M		
Extra drain plug	L		
Raw water pump impeller (if applicable) with necessary tools	M	X	If you can get at this pump from above the water, bring a spare
Spare bulbs for navigation lights and search lights	M		
rags	M		When making emergency fixes to the engine or bilge, you will often find yourself with dirty hands. You will want to be able to clean your hands with rags and hand cleaner.
Waterless hand cleaner	M		For greasy hands
Emergency			

Hull containment mat Damage control mat Collision mat	H		This is a triangle-shaped canvas or nylon used to drape over a hole in the hull. Tie it on as best you can. It will slow down the water intake and possibly keep your boat afloat until help arrives.
Sea anchor	H		
Mylar space blanket	H		The larger versions are capable of sheltering 2 people inside. Two people will stay much warmer than one.
First aid kit	H		
Wool blankets	H		Wool is good at keeping in body heat, even when it gets wet. Wool is also inherently flame retardant. You can use

				it as an additional means of putting out fires.
	Emergency hooded rain poncho	M		If you don't have rain gear for each passenger, these might come in handy and they are cheap.
	Nylon tow line or strap	H		
	Coast Guard-required safety Equip PFDs, flares, etc.	H		
	Bucket, at least 2 gallons	H		
	Emergency metal fuel tank with fuel line	L	X	If you are sure you will not run out of fuel and that your fuel will not be contaminated, you will not need this.
	Emergency position indicating radio beacon (EPIRB)		X	Needed for long cruises
	Life raft(s)		X	
Equipment				
	Portable lighting	H		This includes multiple types and

			configurations of flashlights and extra copies of their power source (batteries).
Radios	H		
Portable VHF	M		
Sounders	H		
Supplies and Equipment	Urgency (H,M,L)	Optional	
Lead line	M		Backup for sounder equipment. Simple line with depth markings and a weight heavy enough to sink the line.
GPS	H		
Charts	H		
Compass	H		
Search light	H		
Ground tackle	H		Includes anchor, anchor rode, etc. Must be in good condition. Check condition of chain or rope.
Redundancy			
Fuel pump	H		

	Raw water pump	H	
	Bilge pumps	H	
	Sounders		
	Navigation data		
	VHF radio		
Apparel			
	Bad weather apparel		
	Wet suit, mask, and snorkel		Used for underwater repair and inspection

A

ABYC · 96, 110
Air Filter · 122

B

bathtub curve · 35, 45, 47
batteries · 75, 85, 86, 87, 104, 119, 130, 150
Battery · 49, 63, 85, 123, 146
bilge monitors · 118
bilge pump · 16, 93, 94, 95, 96, 98, 100, 101, 102, 103, 104, 105, 106, 107, 116, 118, 127, 138, 139
Bilge Pump Switch · 105
bilge pump system · 96, 101, 106
bilge pumps · 93, 94, 95, 97, 100, 101, 102, 103, 106
bilge system · 26, 86, 96, 100, 101, 102, 103, 107, 117
biocides · 74
bonding system · 110, 111, 112

C

charging system · 84
Clogging Indicator · 122
Coast Guard · 16, 22, 29, 30
Conformal coating · 79, 82
contaminated fuel · 78, 118
corrosion · 28, 61, 65, 72, 81, 82, 85, 92
cylinder head water temperature · 71
Cylinder head water temperature · 69

D

dielectric compound · 81, 84
dielectric compounds · 80, 81
dielectric film · 79

dielectric grease · 28, 72, 78, 80, 81, 82, 85, 92
Disasters · 17

E

early warning sensors · 68
Emergencies · 17
Emergency · 85, 95, 106, 107, 125, 128
emergency bilge pump · 26, 103
Emergency Pumps · 106
engine failure · 65
Engine temperature · 119
Ewen Thompson · 107, 110
exhaust boot · 97
exhaust gas temperature · 70
exhaust manifold · 67, 68, 70, 91, 120
exhaust manifold surface temperature · 68
exhaust riser surface temperature · 68

F

Filter Clogging Indicators · 122
fire · 23, 28, 29, 62, 63, 77, 78, 81, 89, 90, 91, 92, 93, 108, 125, 126, 127, 141
flexible impeller pump · 66
flood · 55, 127
Flood · 138
FMEA · 52, 53, 54, 58, 143
FMEA Process · 52
FMRA · 58, 59, 60
fuel contamination · 72, 73, 74
Fuel Filter · 72
fuel filters · 73, 74, 75, 76, 122
fuel pump · 76
fuel system monitoring · 76

G

generator · 81, 84, 85
GPS · 22, 23, 28, 81, 117, 123, 126, 151
grounding system · 110

153

H

heat exchangers · 70
high water alarm · 94, 104, 105, 106, 107, 116, 118
High Water Alarm · 106
hull fittings · 26, 96, 97, 98, 102, 128, 141

K

Kedging · 136
kidney loop filtration · 75

L

lightning · 79, 107, 108, 109, 110, 111, 112, 138
Loran · 22, 60, 123, 139

M

man overboard · 127
marine electronics · 80
Marine starters · 78
Miss Majestic · 100, 102, 144
monitoring · 34, 67, 69, 70, 76, 80, 117, 119, 123
MTBF · 18, 35, 40, 47
Murphy's Law · 137
Murpy's Law · 19

N

Navigation · 63, 123
Navy · 130, 132
Normal reliability · 18

O

Oil Filter · 122
Over-voltage · 79

P

Panther · 93, 94
PFDs · 25, 89, 90, 102, 140
planning · 17, 26, 33, 34, 51, 54, 125, 126, 127
points and condenser · 71
power spikes · 79
Propulsion Reliability · 48
prove your boat · 138

Q

Questar · 15, 16, 33, 73, 127

R

Rate of a leak from a One Inch Hole · 99
raw cooling water · 65, 120, 141
raw cooling water monitoring · 69
Raw water cooling system · 97
Raw water flow rate. · 68
redundancy · 28, 42, 43, 45, 47, 58, 59, 63, 78, 85, 86, 102, 104, 127, 139, 140
Redundancy · 38, 45, 47, 62, 63, 85, 107, 139
riser · 67, 68, 69, 120
risk management · 54
rudder · 26, 78, 95, 130, 135, 136
run aground · 93
running aground · 135

S

Seastreak · 90
sinking · 23, 27, 55, 62, 63, 94, 95, 97, 106, 107, 116, 125, 126
SONAR · 98
standby redundant · 39, 45, 46, 47, 48
starter motor · 42, 72, 78, 84, 140
Steering · 78, 131
surface temperature monitoring · 70

T

The Morning Dew · 22
thunder · 107, 108, 109, 112
thunderstorms · 107, 108
tools · 59, 71, 72, 146

U

US Coast Guard · 16

V

VHF radio · 16, 139
voltage regulator · 28, 81

W

water - separators · 74
Water in the fuel · 118
water removal · 74
wax formation · 75

www.ingramcontent.com/pod-product-compliance
Lightning Source LLC
Chambersburg PA
CBHW050554300426
44112CB00013B/1911